AF496441

NO JOY WITHOUT
Scotland

Photographs of Scotland

by

James Trueman

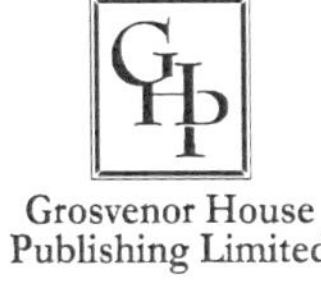

Grosvenor House
Publishing Limited

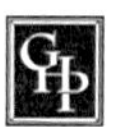

This book is published by
Grosvenor House Publishing Ltd
Link House
140 The Broadway, Tolworth, Surrey, KT6 7HT.
www.grosvenorhousepublishing.co.uk

A CIP record for this book
is available from the British Library

ISBN 978-1-80381-765-1

Foreword by Christine Trueman

It is difficult to explain why Scotland took my breath away as it did. I had never thought that I would want to visit it so often.

After many years of hearing about its spectacular beauty from my son, I accompanied him to several places towards the Western Isles.

Having been twice, I know I shall return again and again. Something about Scotland stole his heart and the same thing has happened to me.

I hope that these photographs will transform your life, too, and make you want to see Scotland with your own eyes.

Christine Trueman

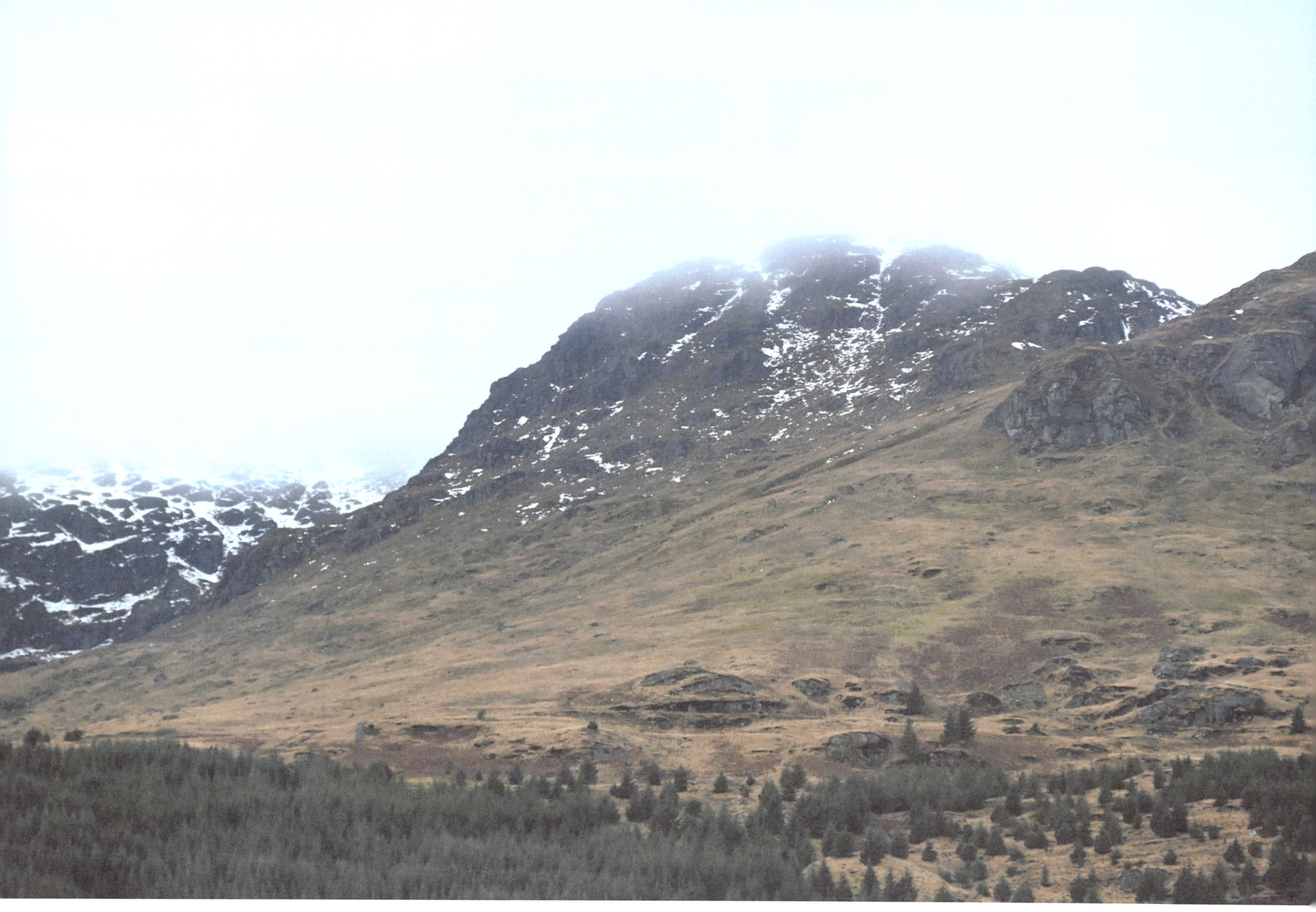

High above wintry Arrochar in the Trossachs National Park, the olive and green crags are laced with snow.

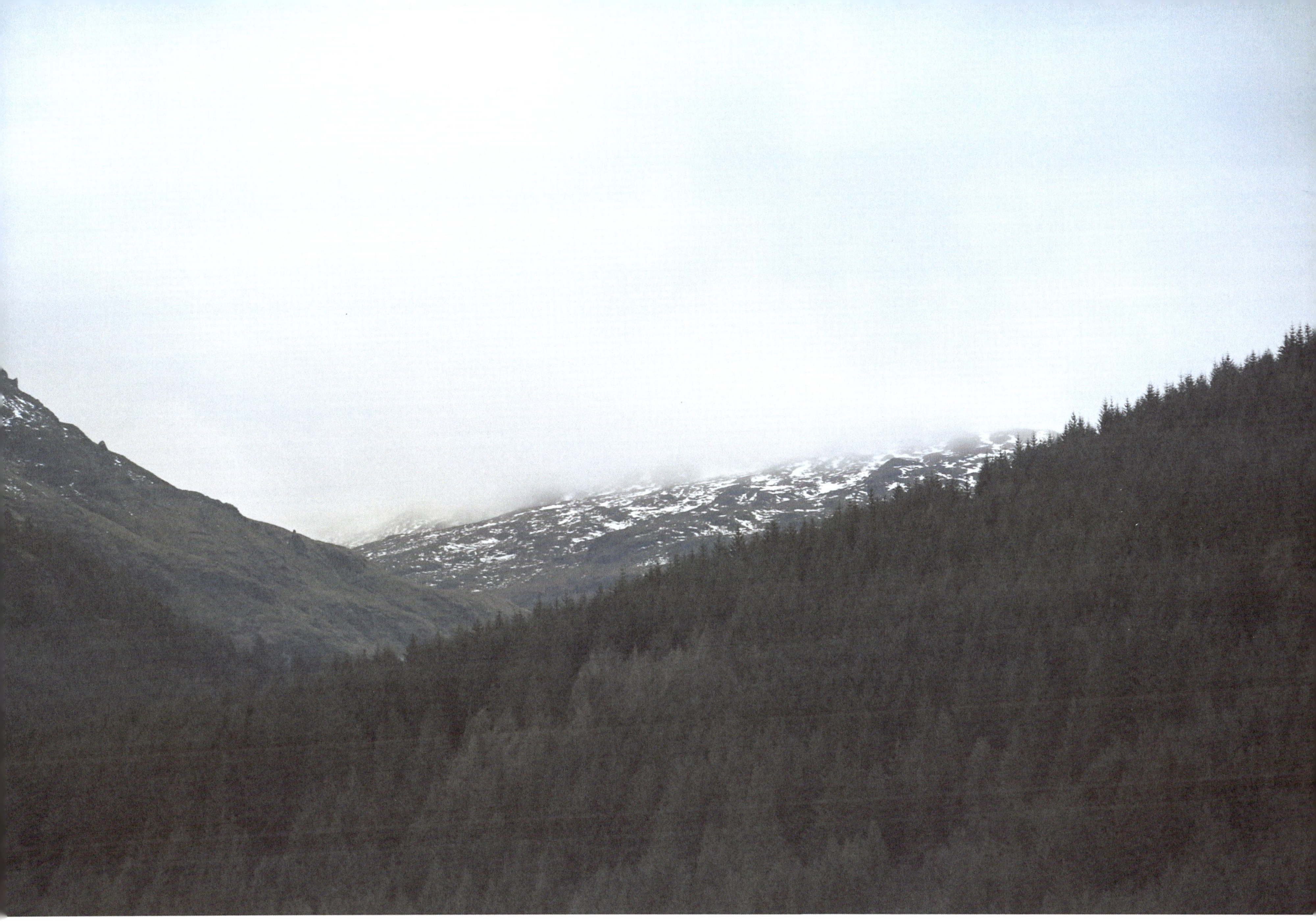

A dense forest of pine trees meets with a valley shrouded in mist.

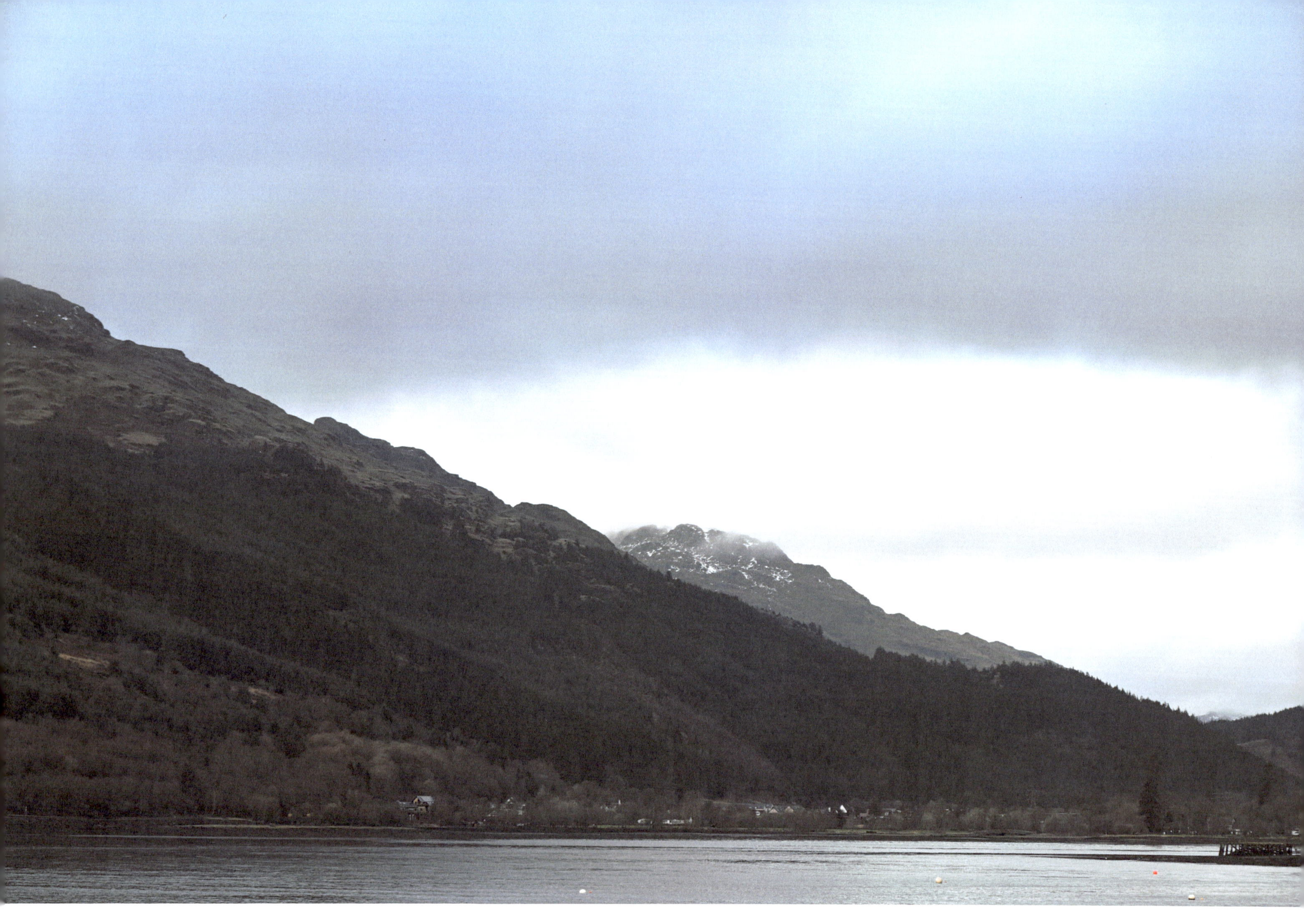

The Arrochar Alps meet with the waters of Loch Long.

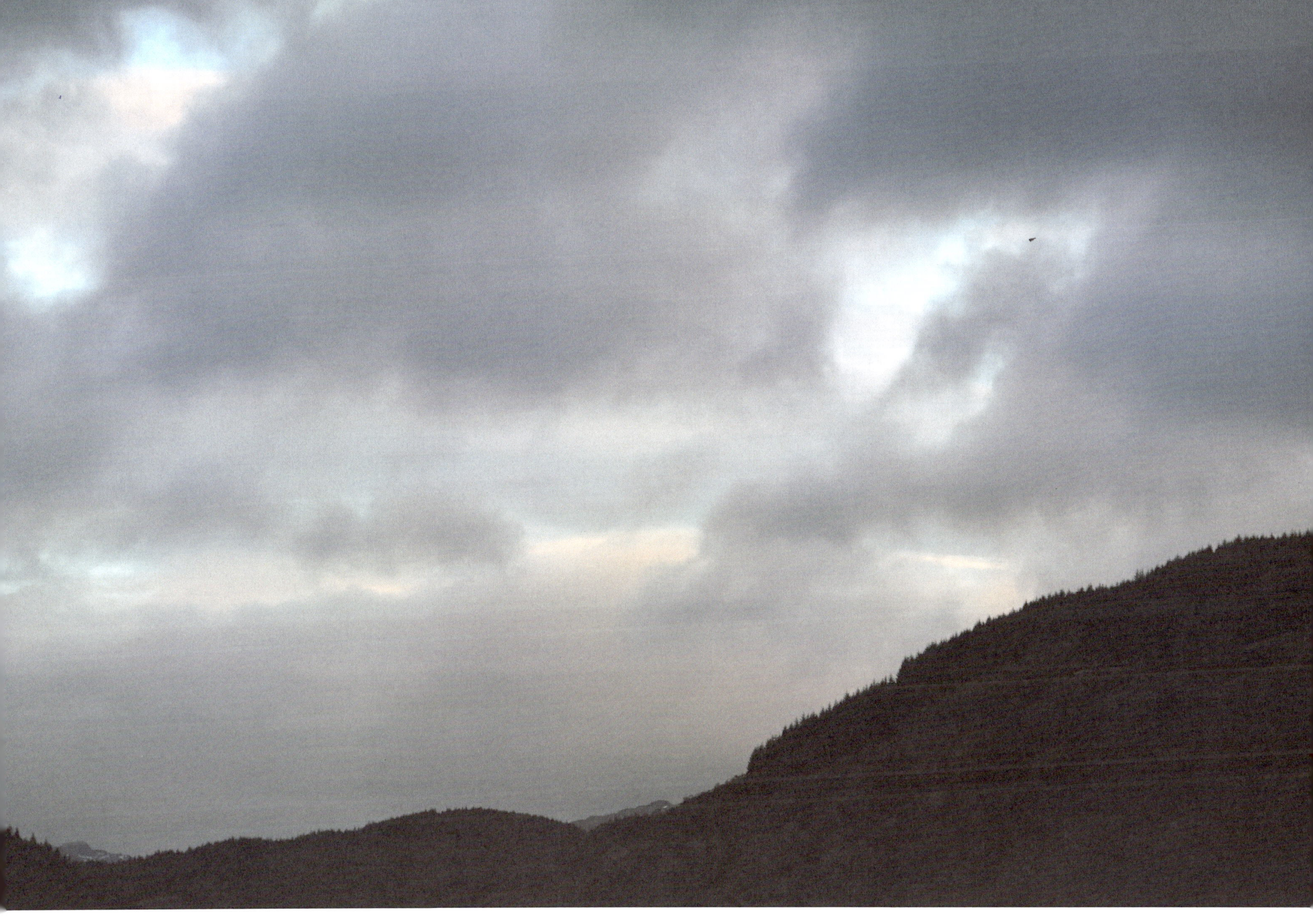

As we leave the Village Inn for an evening walk, the rain clouds gather above us.

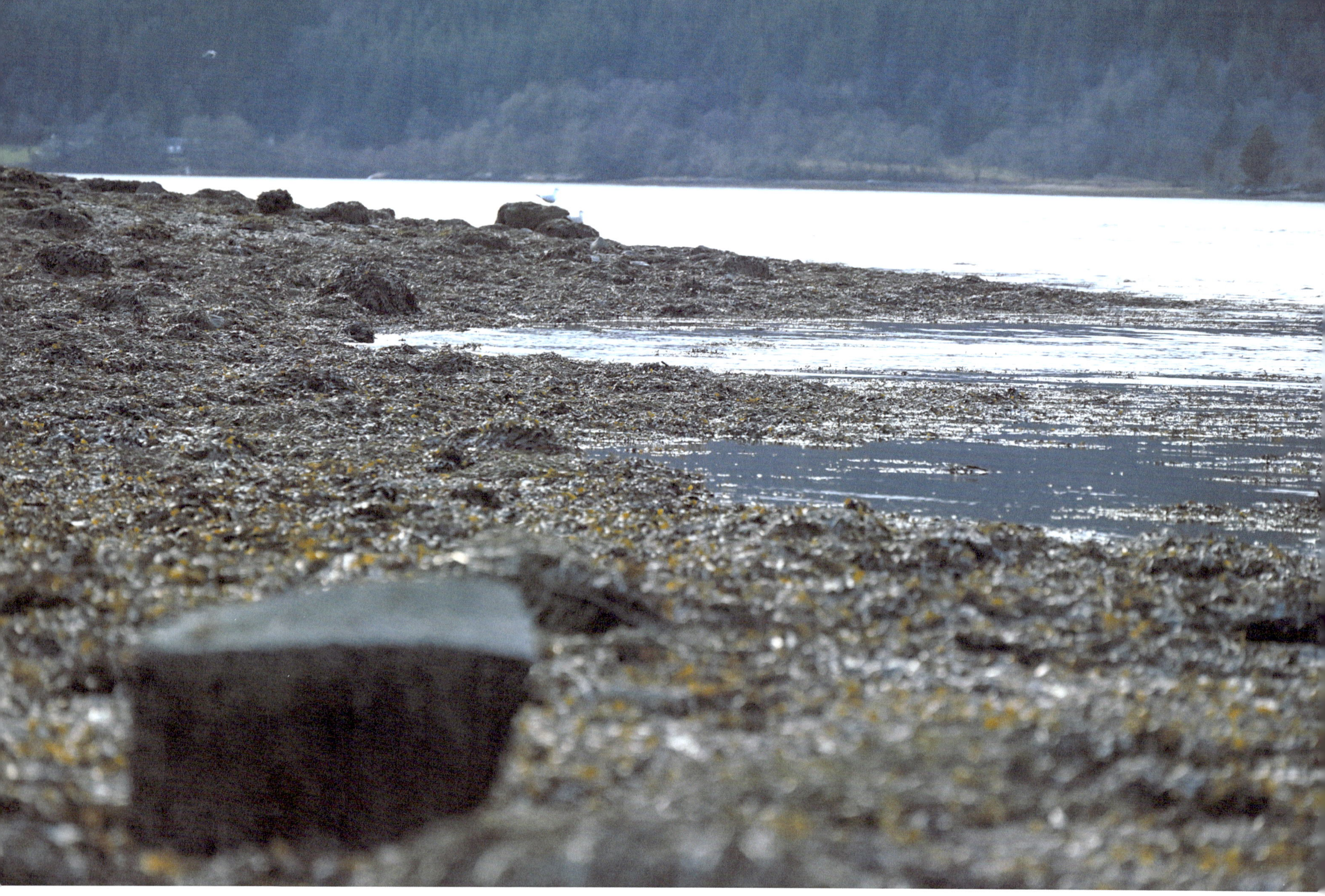

Arrochar, home of the MacFarlane chiefs. The tomb in the churchyard is ghostly beneath MacFarlane's lantern, the pale, white moon. In the morning, the winter sun shines whilst gulls gather on a weed-strewn shore.

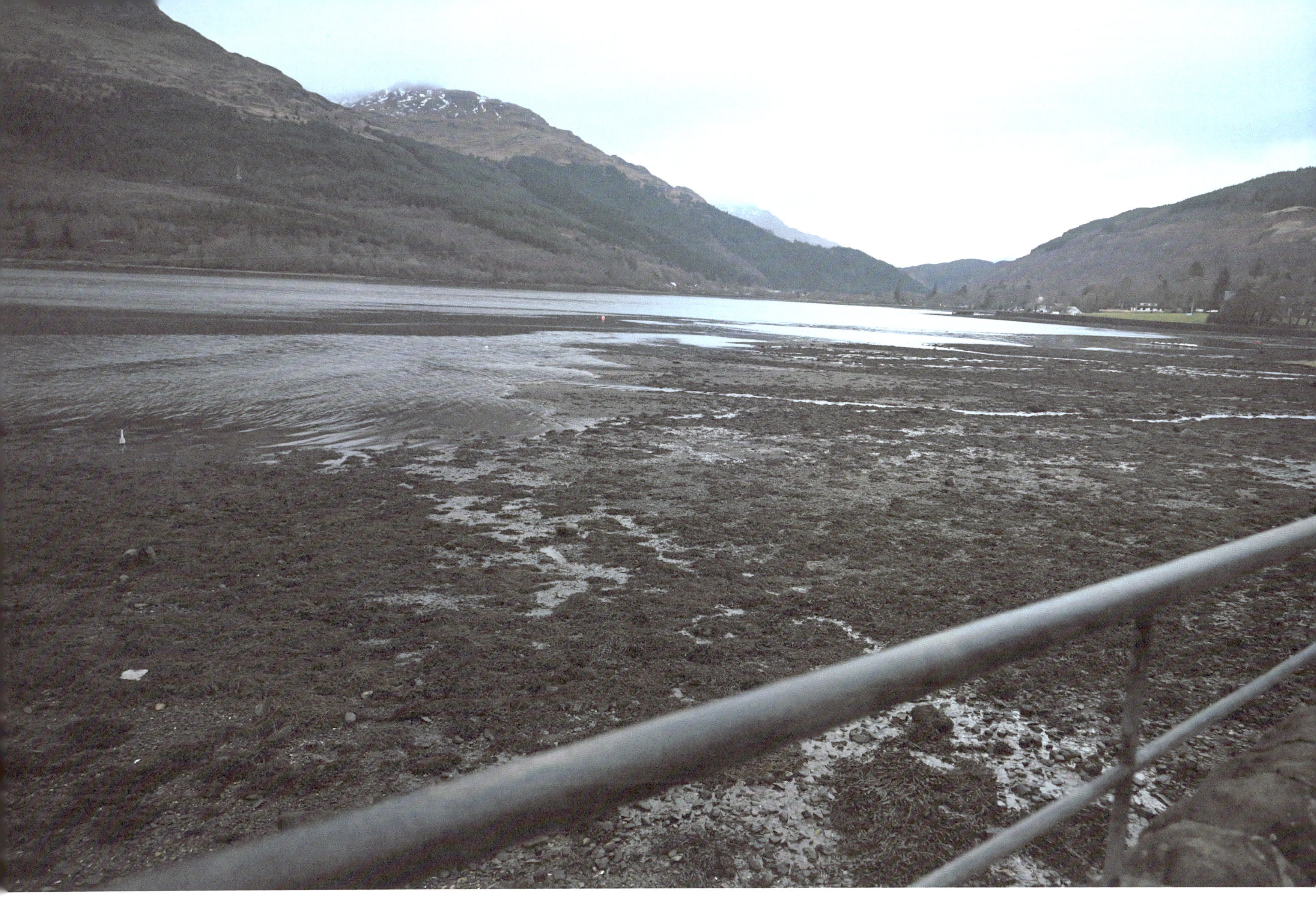

A picture taken from the sea wall. The loch winds into the distance towards the River Loin.
Legend has it that Robert the Bruce hid in the Glen Loin caves after his army's defeat in 1306.

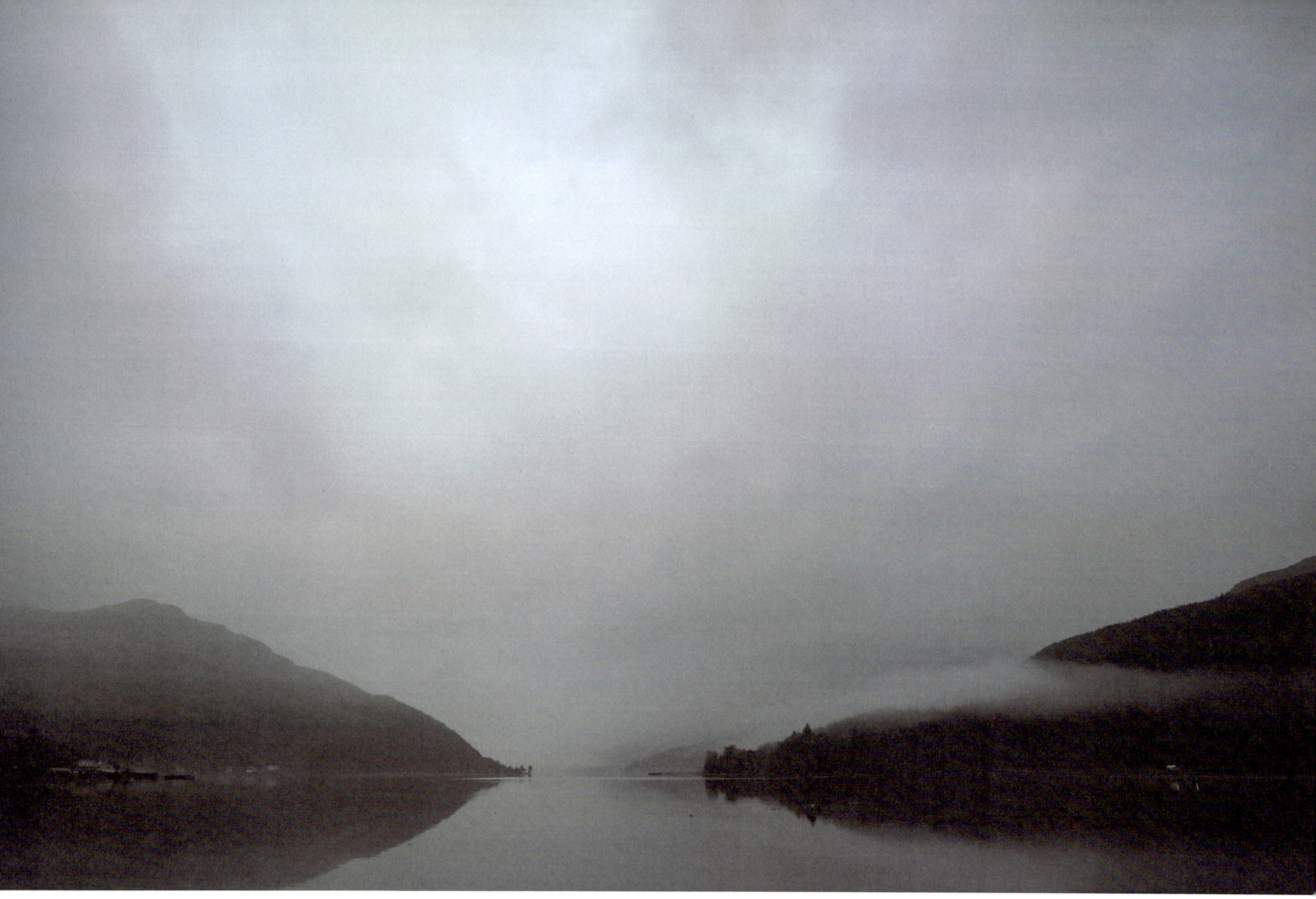

Mist floats like a dragon's breath, hiding the distant loch. I thought of the Lady of the Lake and wondered whether the legendary King Arthur that I associated with Cornwall could have been the very real Somerled, Lord of the Isles?

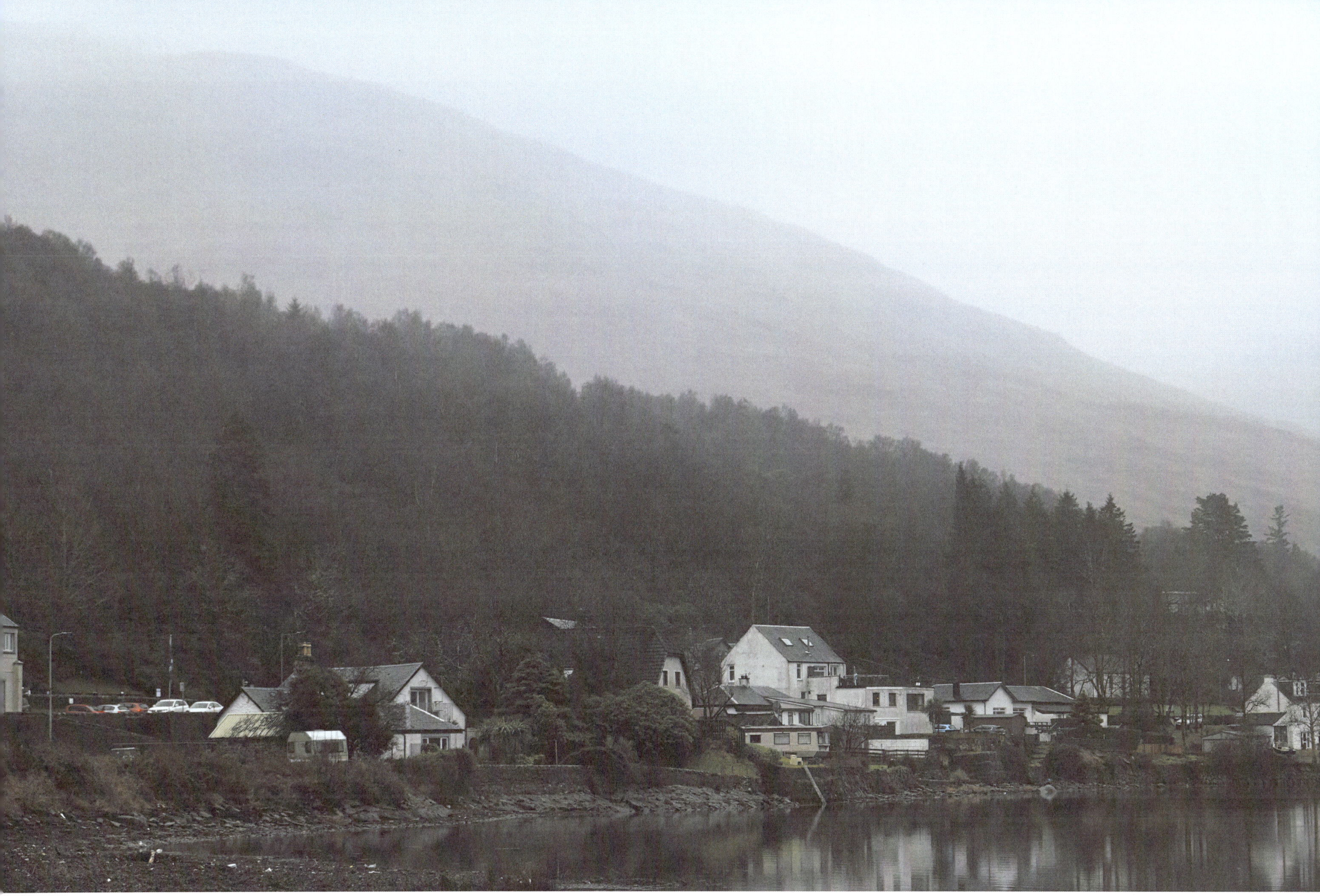

Arrochar, sheltered by the mountains.

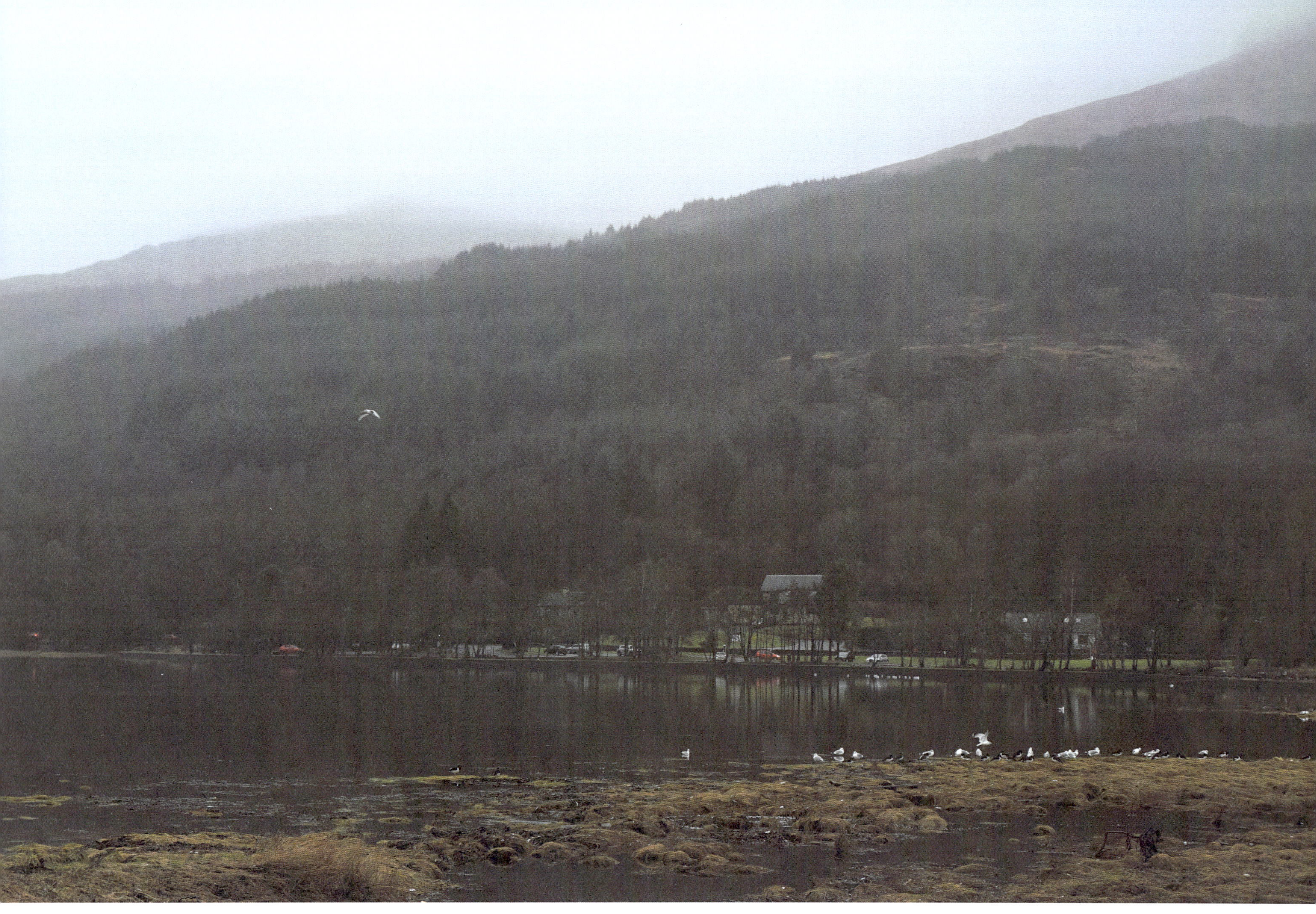

Pale as a cobweb or smoke from a fire, mist cloaks the trees.

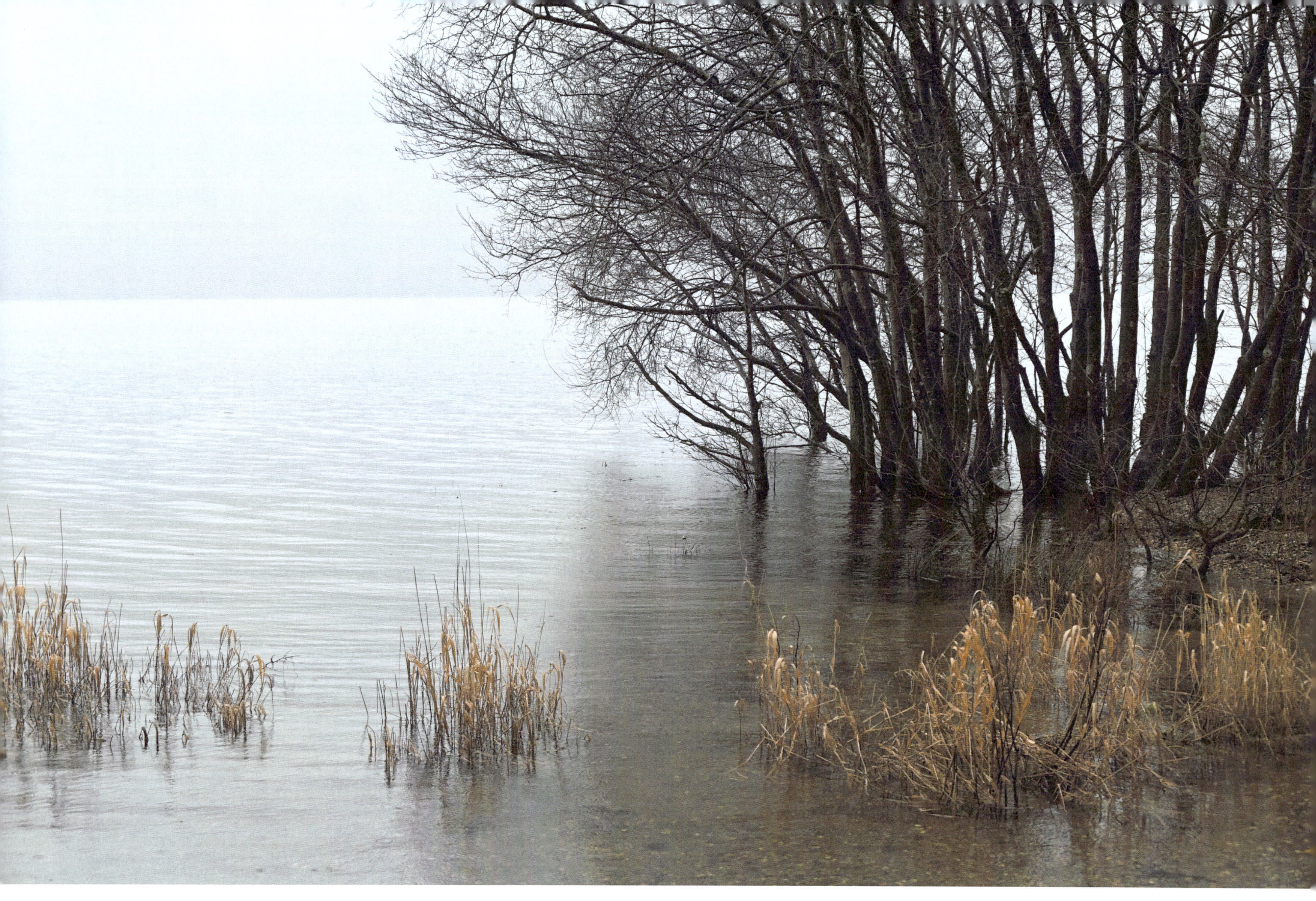

Trees submerged by water at the edge of Loch Lomond.

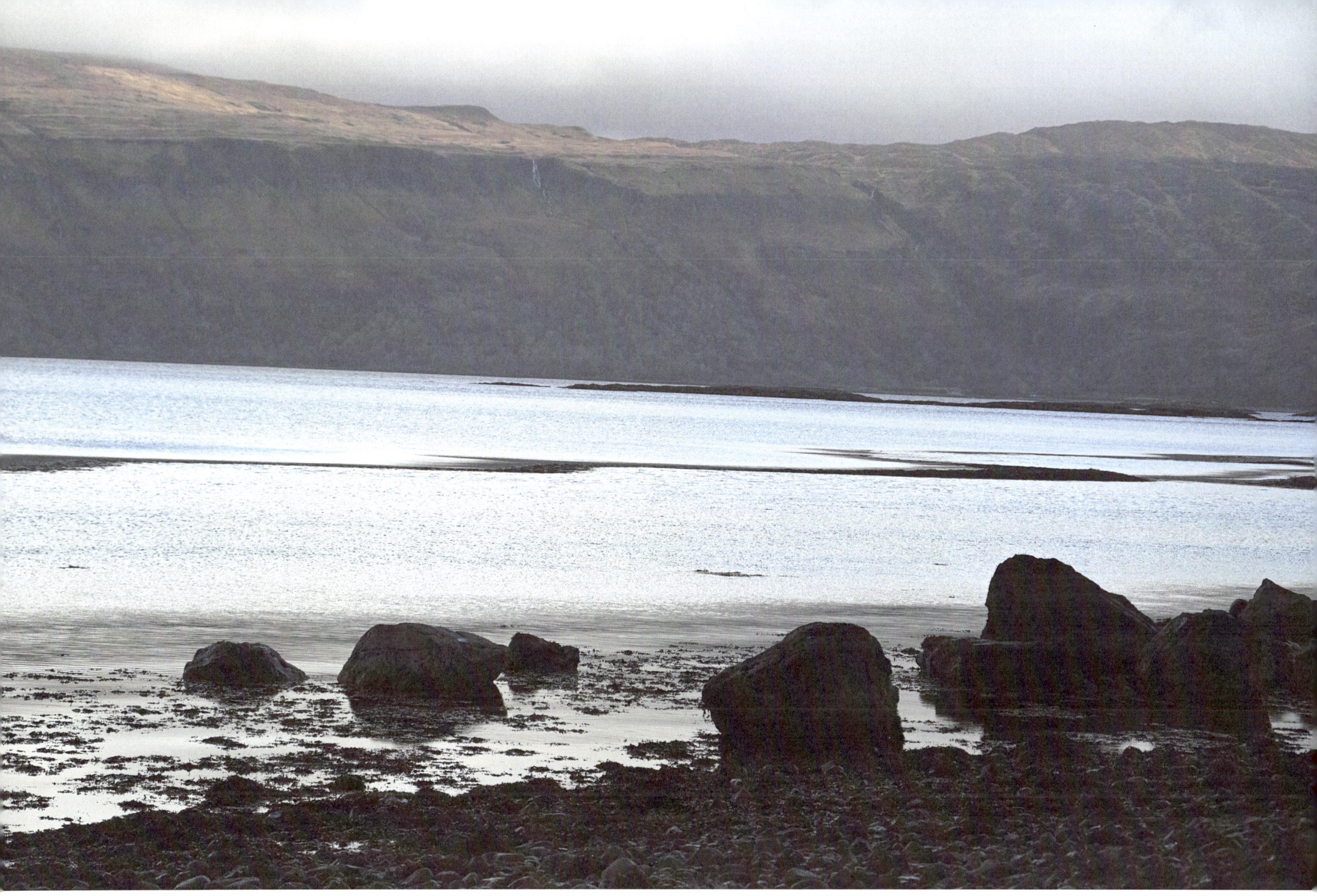

We travel on the Calmac Ferry from Oban to Mull. At Craignure we are met
by the changing colours of the island landscape.

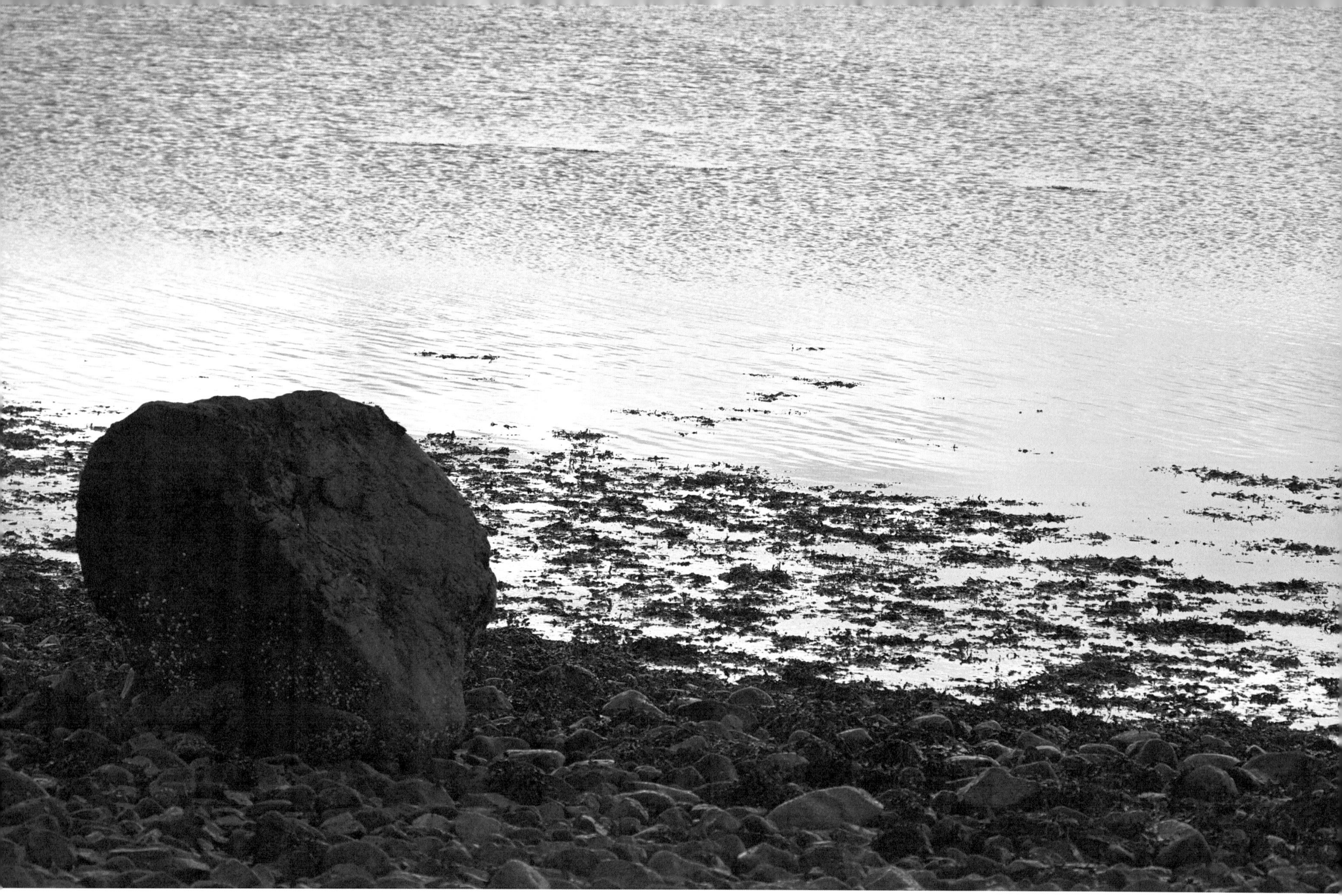

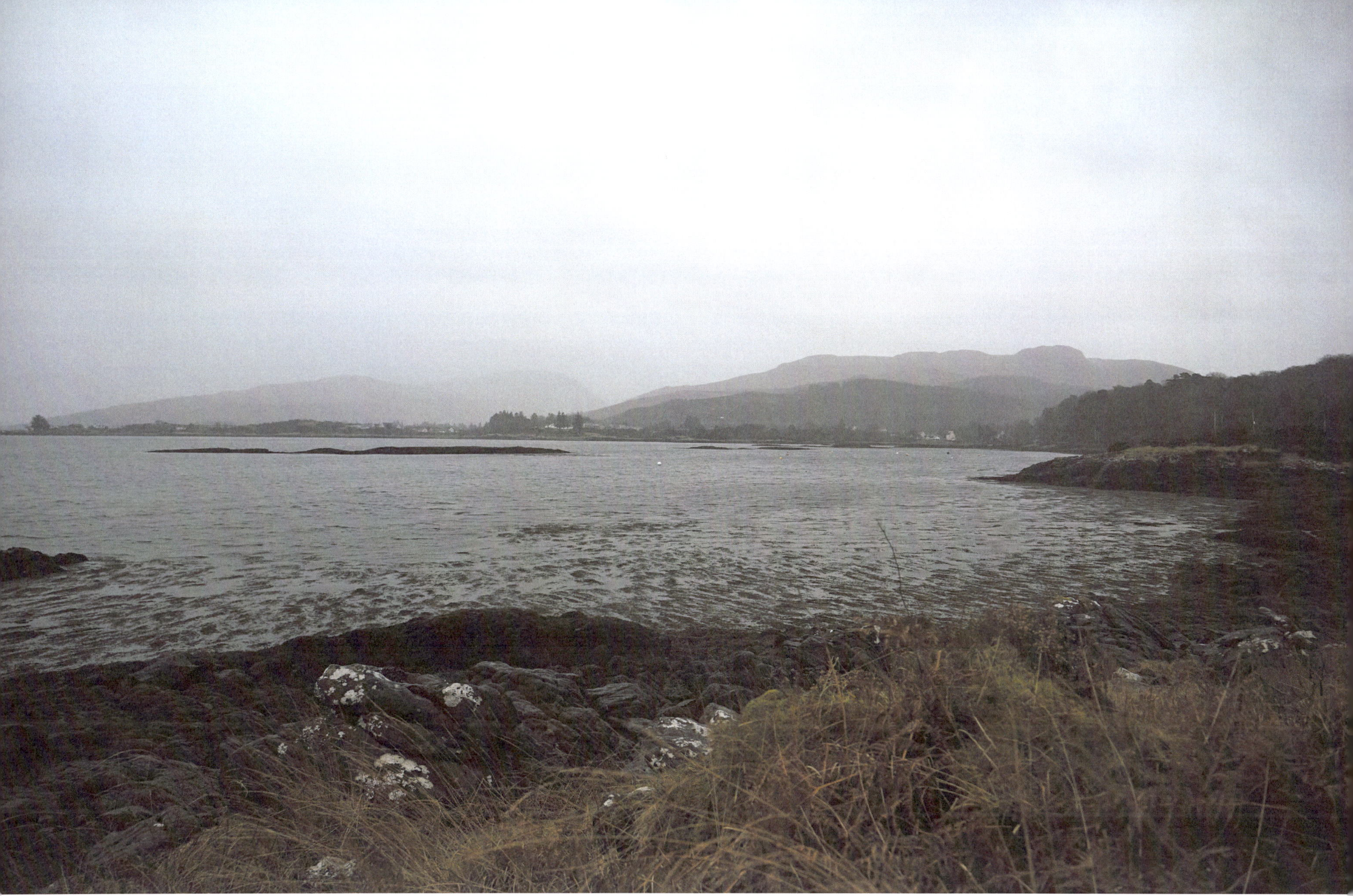

We follow the road to Tobermory from Craignure, a short journey along the coast passing beaches and green-blue rock pools. The road signs say *Otters crossing for the next six miles* and there are no traffic jams – bliss! I think of the numbers of small deer and foxes killed around my home in Oxford and wonder why we have no road signs to protect the wildlife.

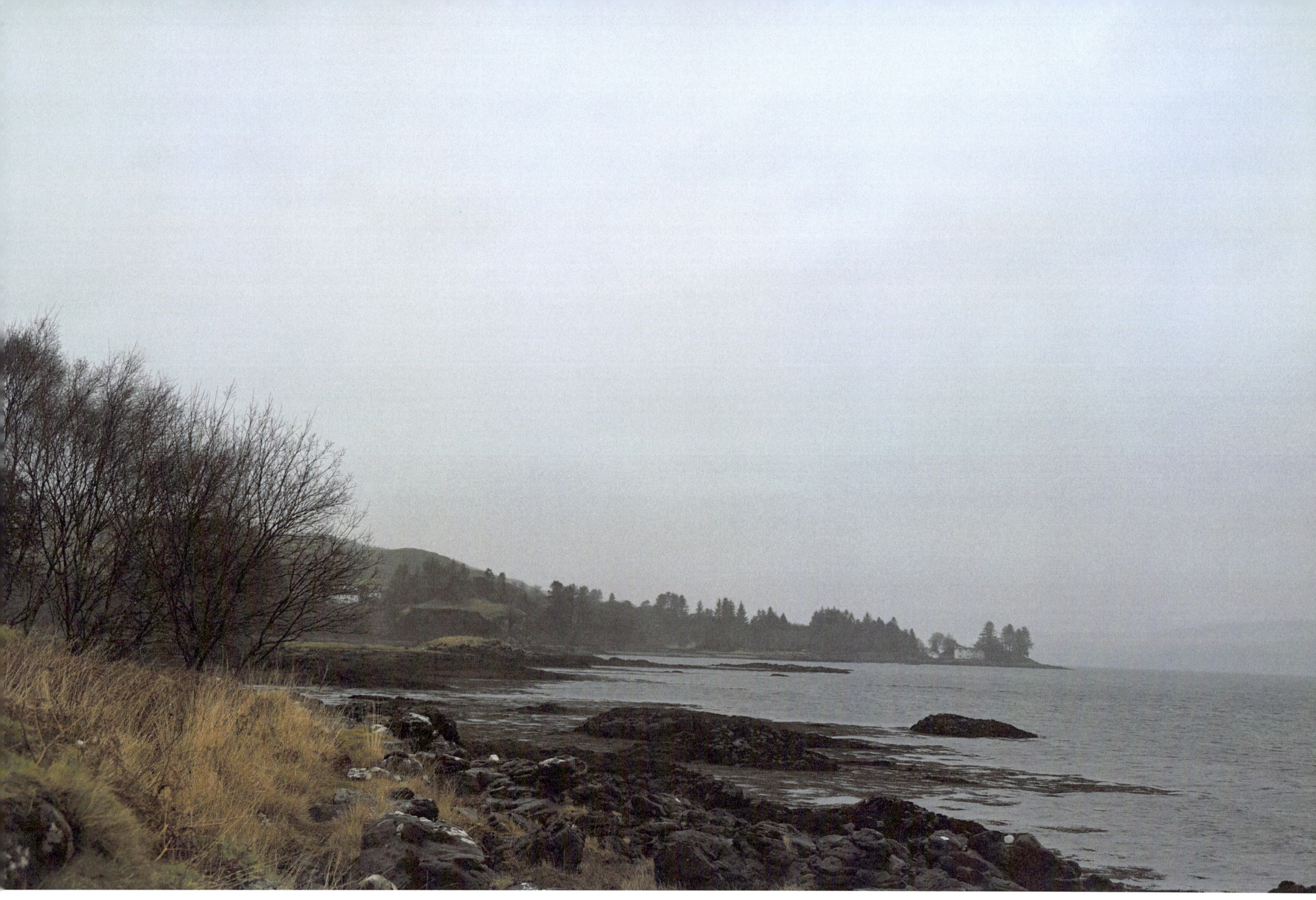

A January landscape. Rocks and trees provide a Gothic backdrop of natural vaults and buttresses.

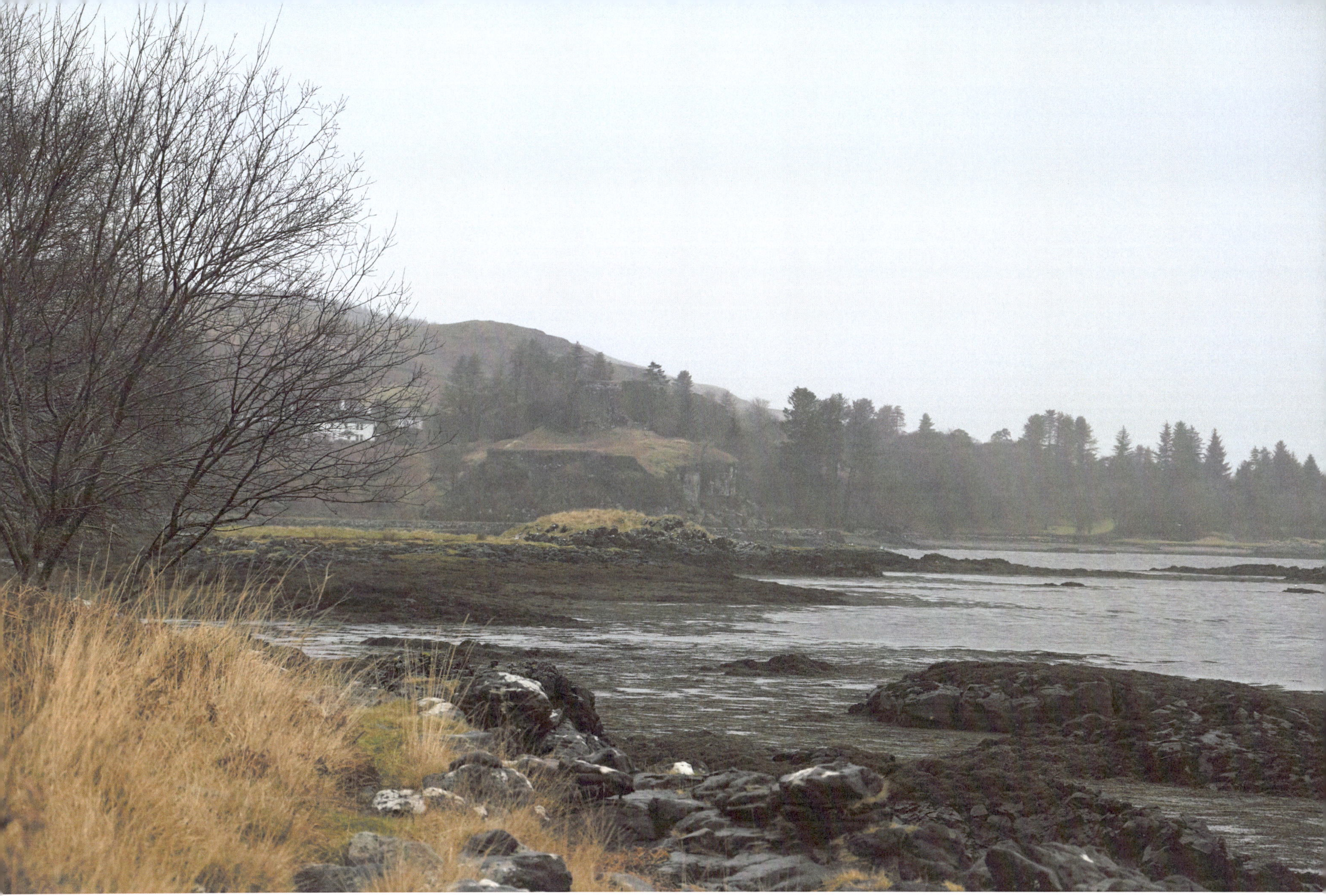

We let Monty the dog out of the car to scamper on the beach and promptly see an otter close to a rock pool. The otter spots the dog and beats a hasty retreat.

A view of the coast of Mull just past the village of Salen.

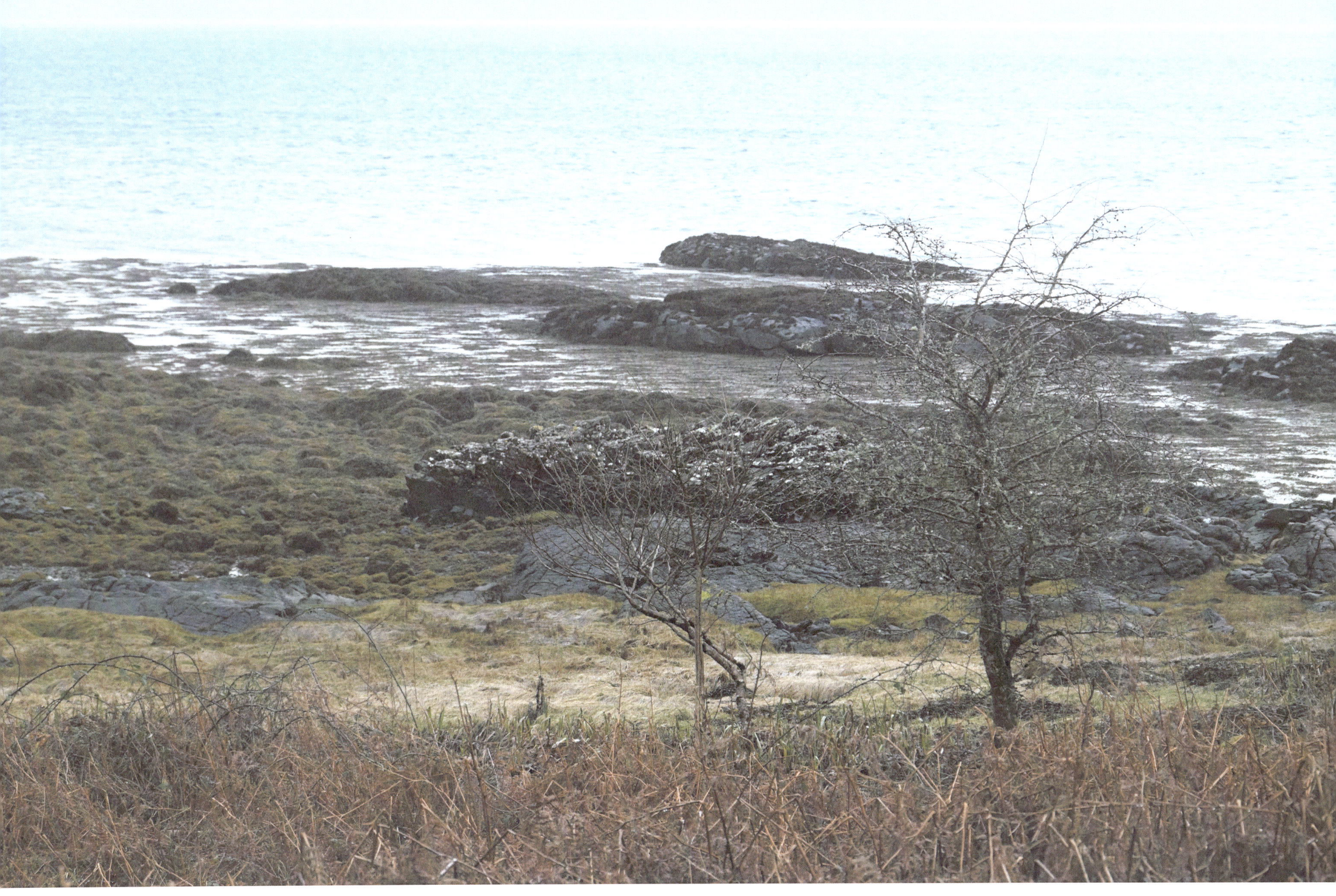

A tangle of trees on the rocky shoreline towards Tobermory.

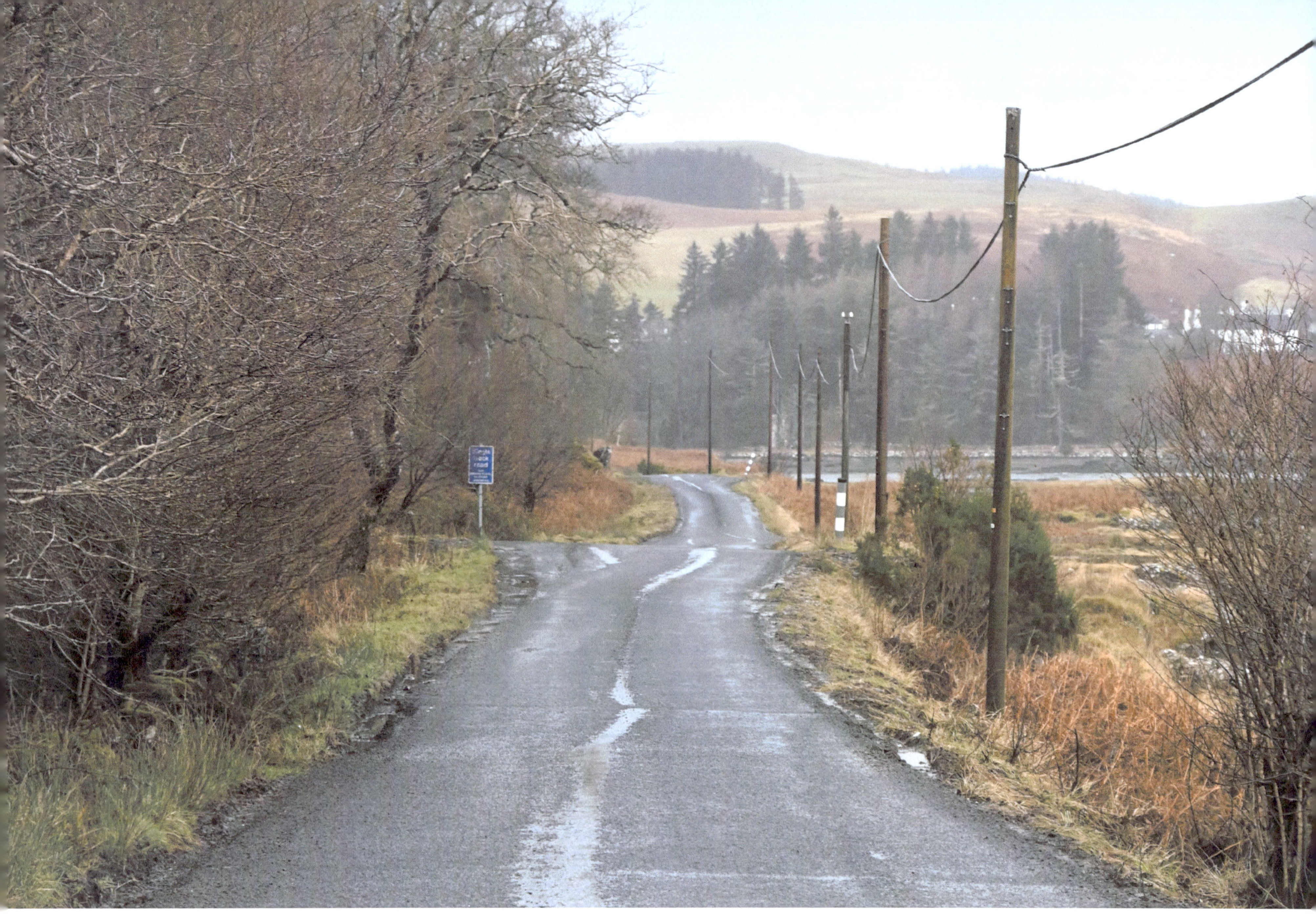

Glorious winter colours.

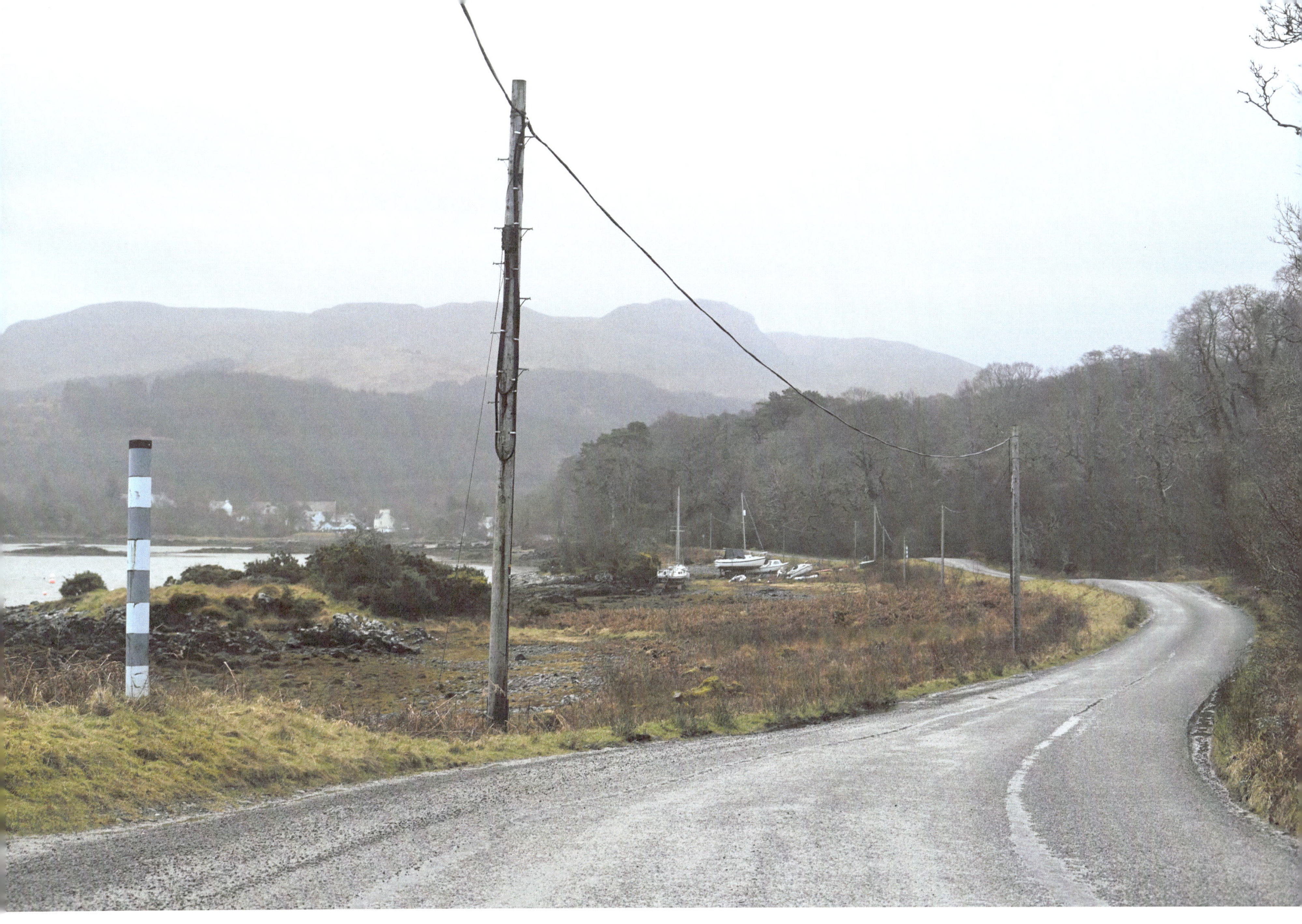

The road to Tobermory. Boats lie upon the shore.

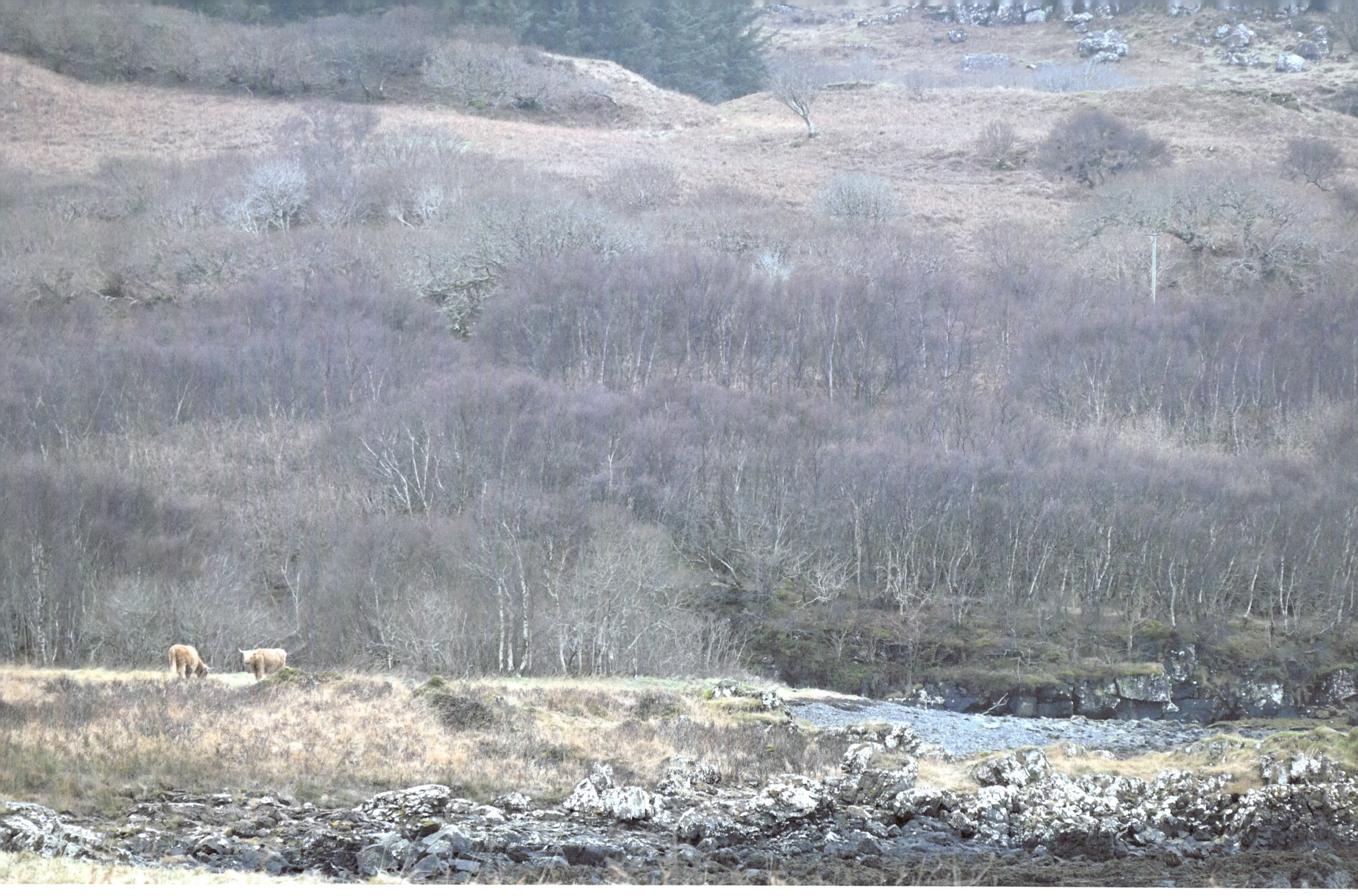

Shaggy island cattle graze peacefully amongst the mauves, golds and greens. We were forced to stop
on several occasions as herds of Highland cattle stood in the road, staring at us in their unhurried way.
They seem so mild, but I wouldn't want to upset them.

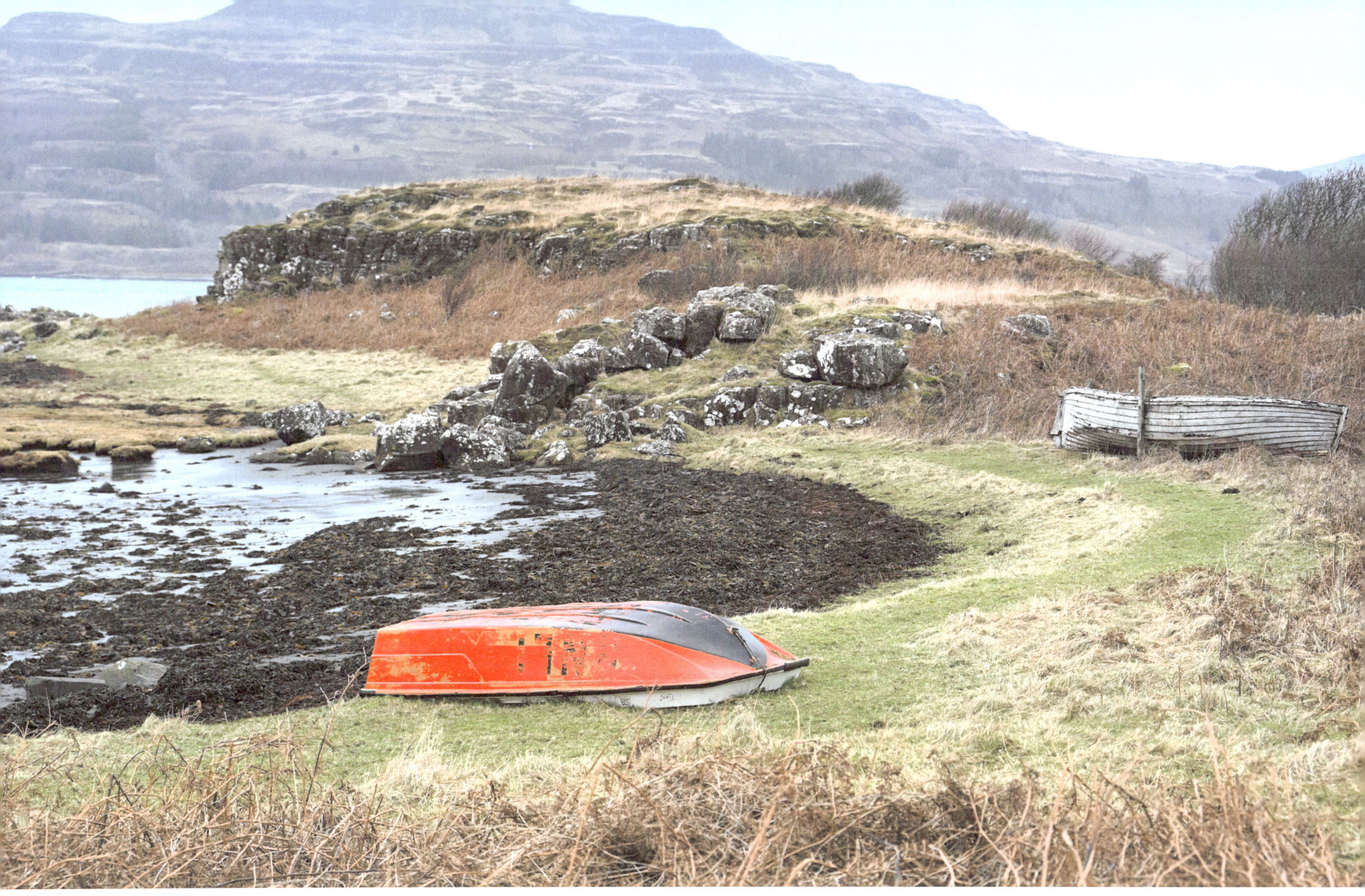

The hull of a red boat makes a vivid splash of colour upon the shore.

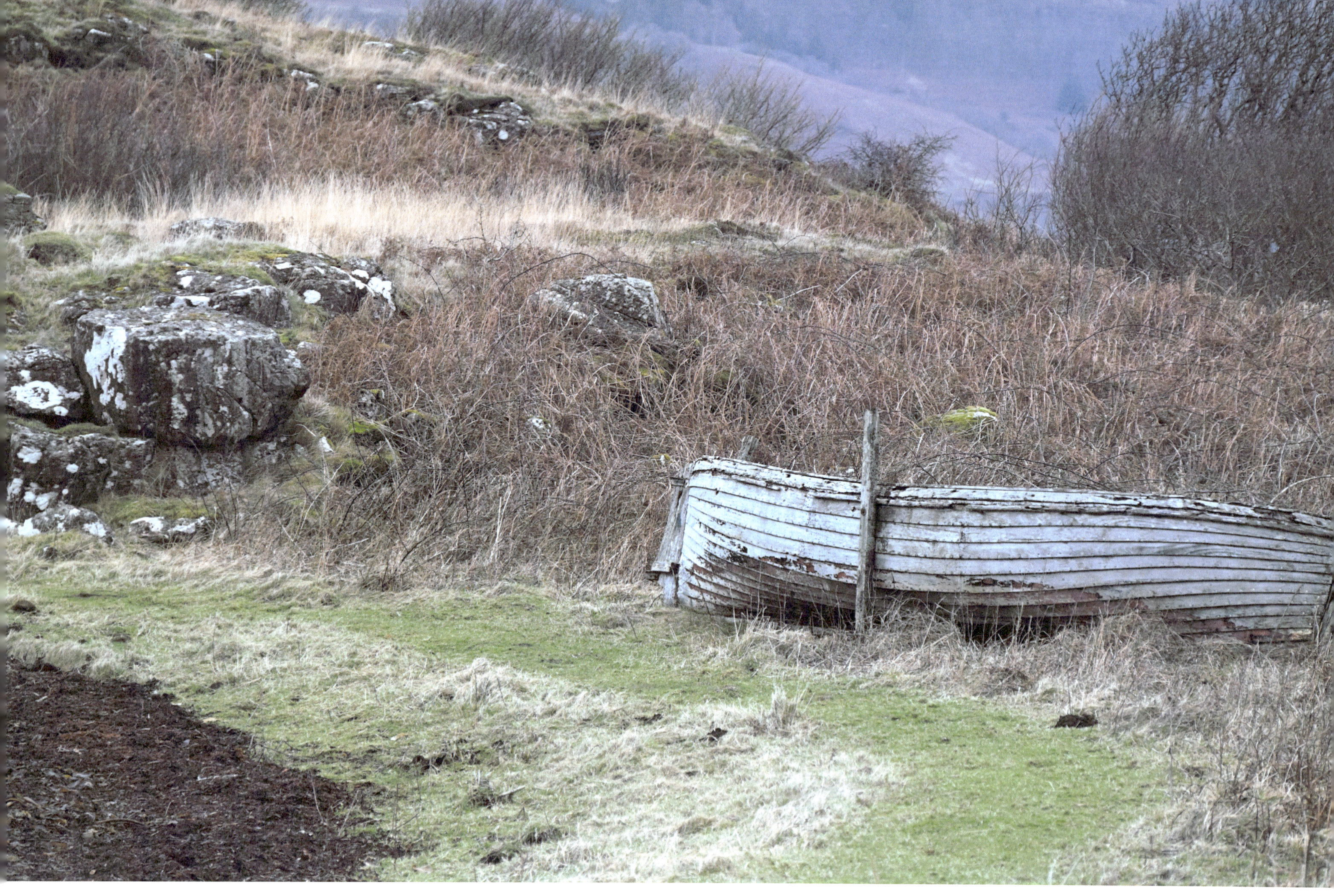

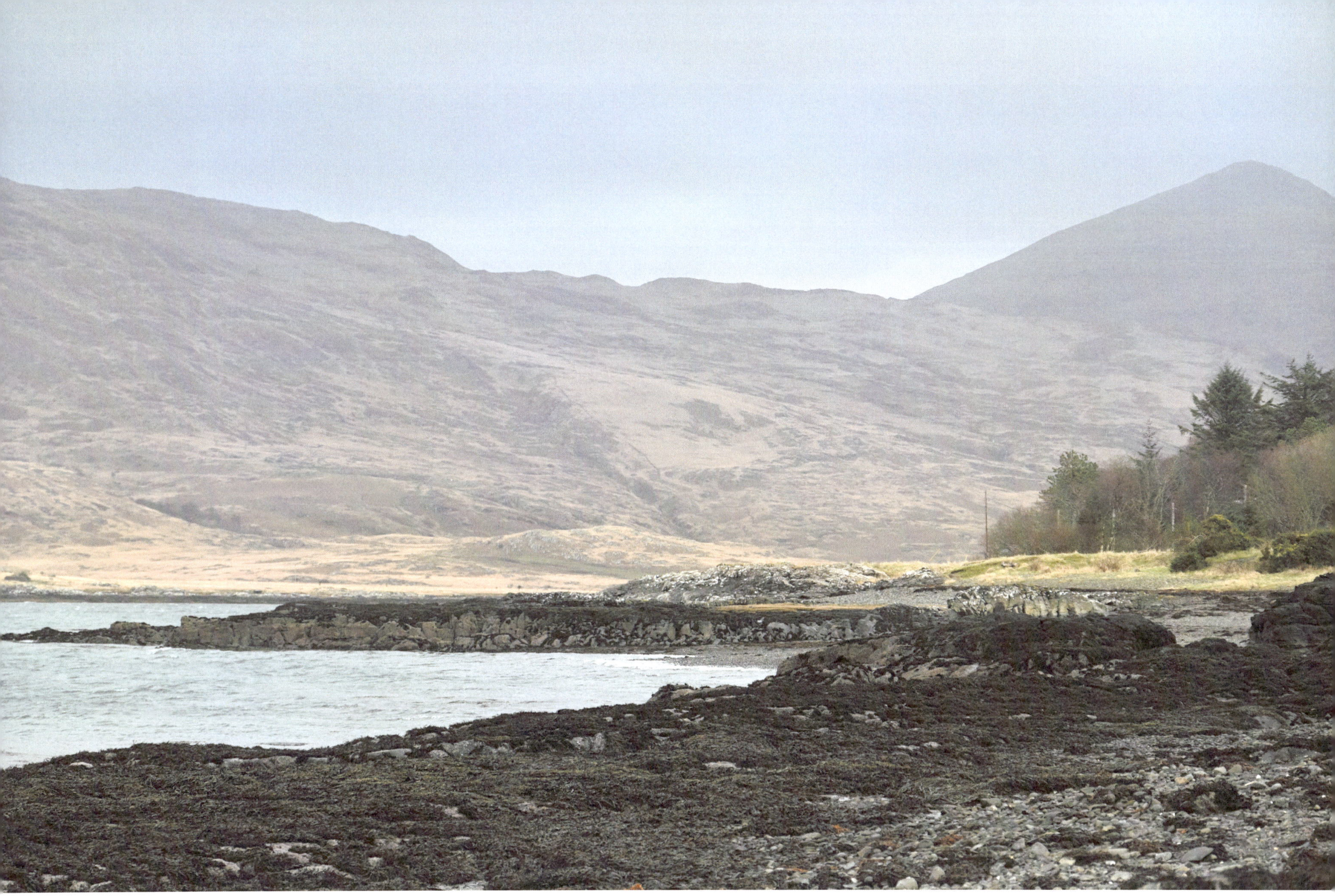

The Mull landscape is often gentle, although the mountains can appear forbidding.
The highest mountain on the island is Ben More.

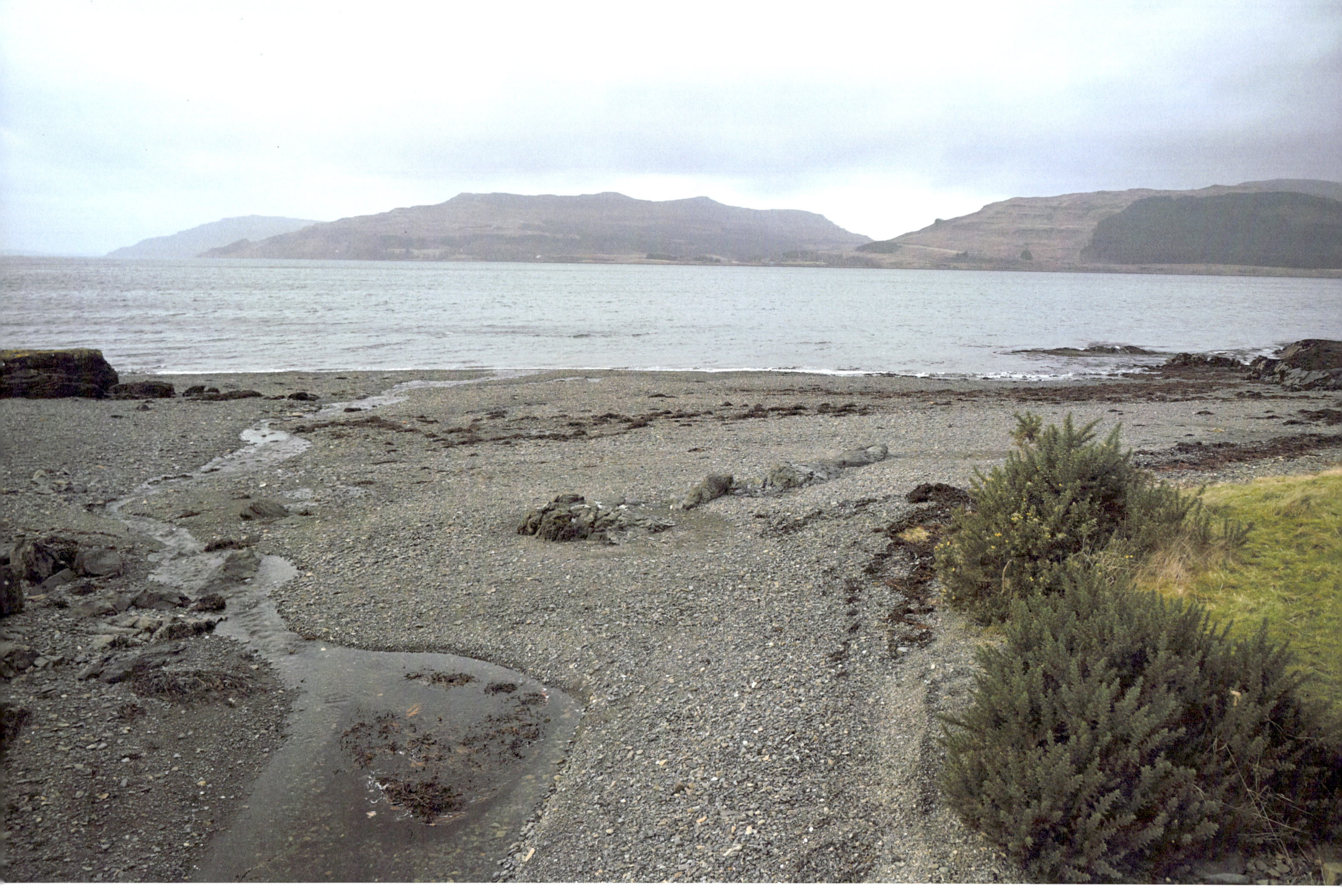

A white beach at Fionnphort opposite Iona and the crystal clear but icy waves between Mull and the island. We had booked the ferry to Iona but were told that the waves were too rough for travel.

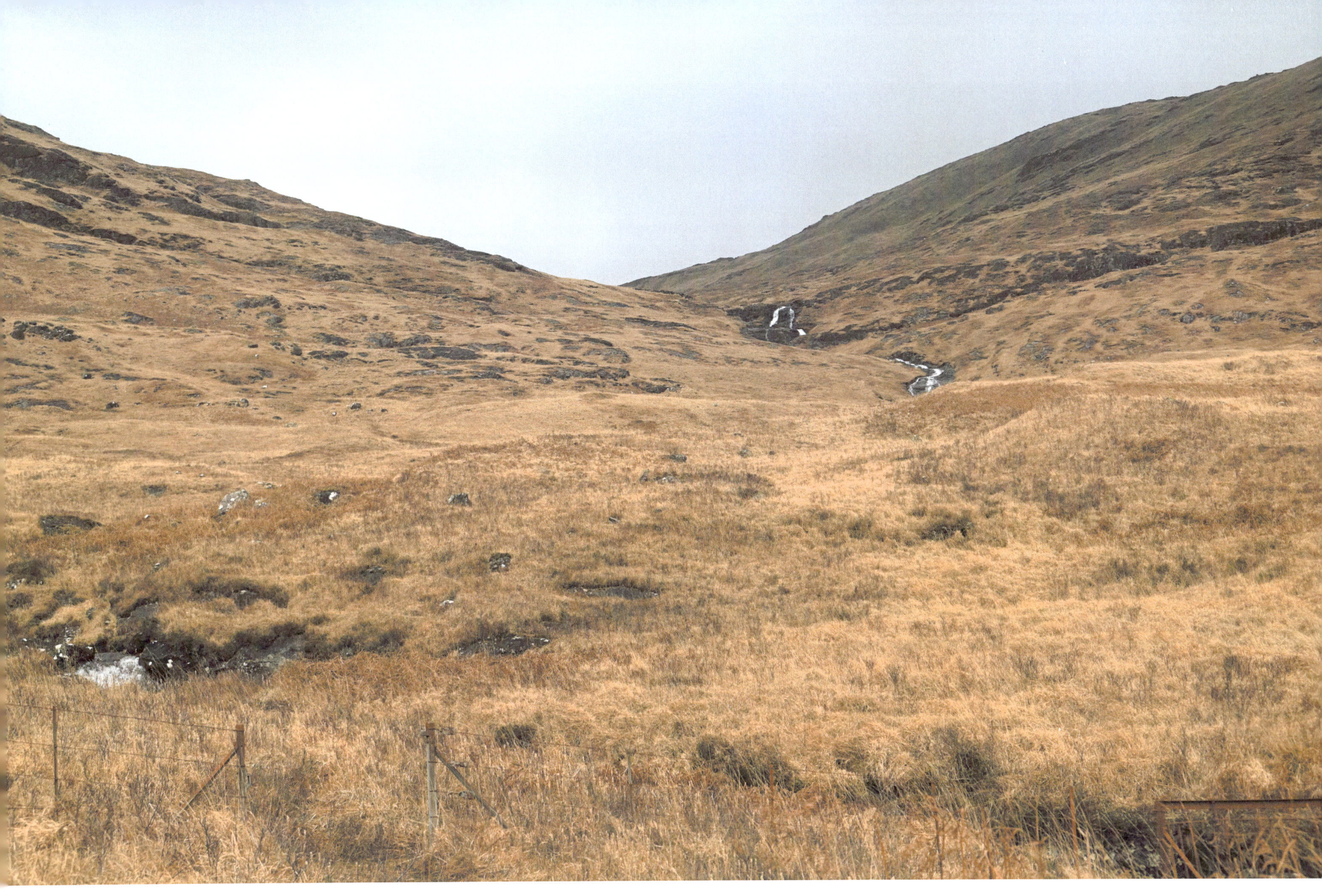

Golden hills close to Fionnphort with a small stream flowing through the distant valley.

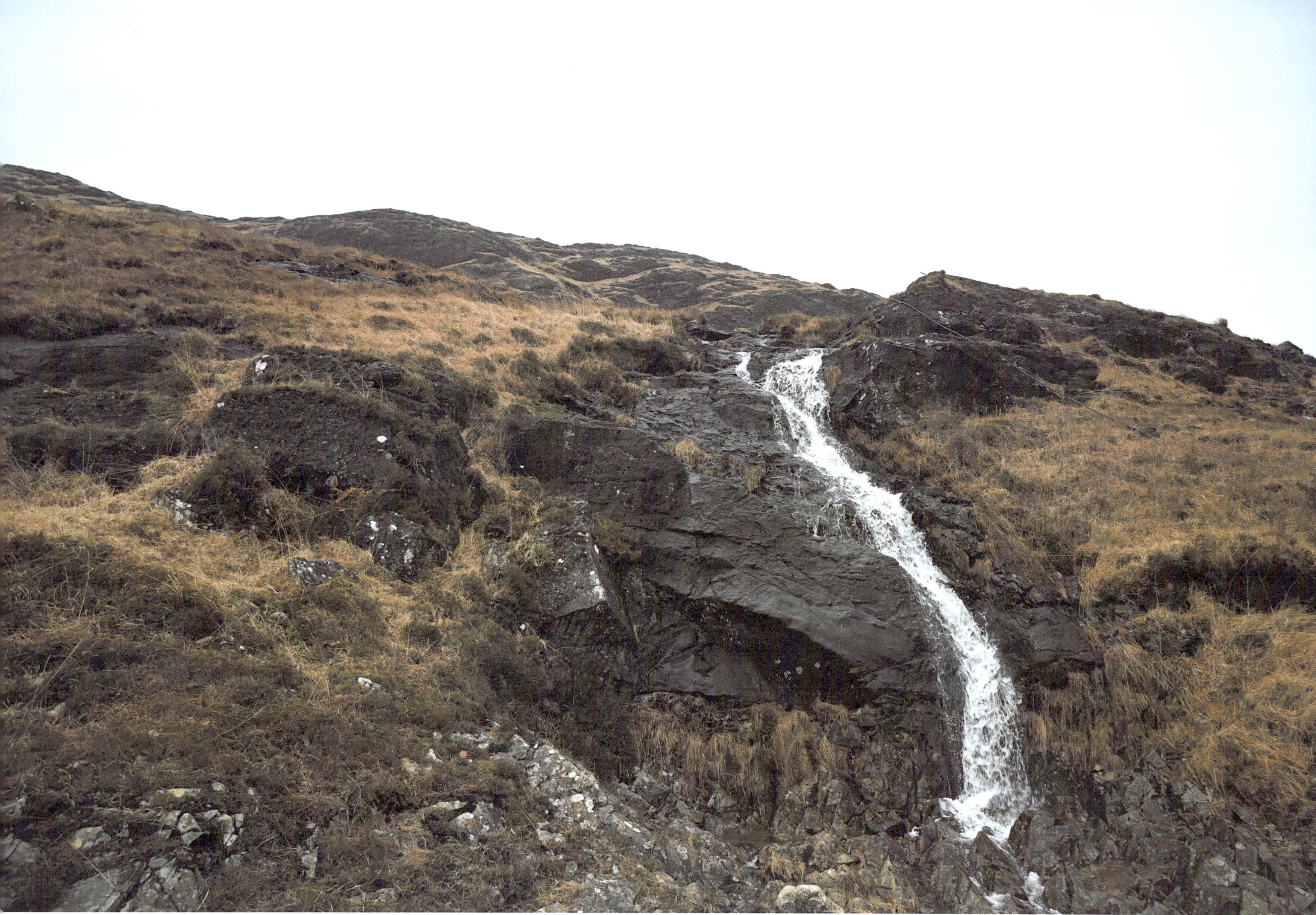

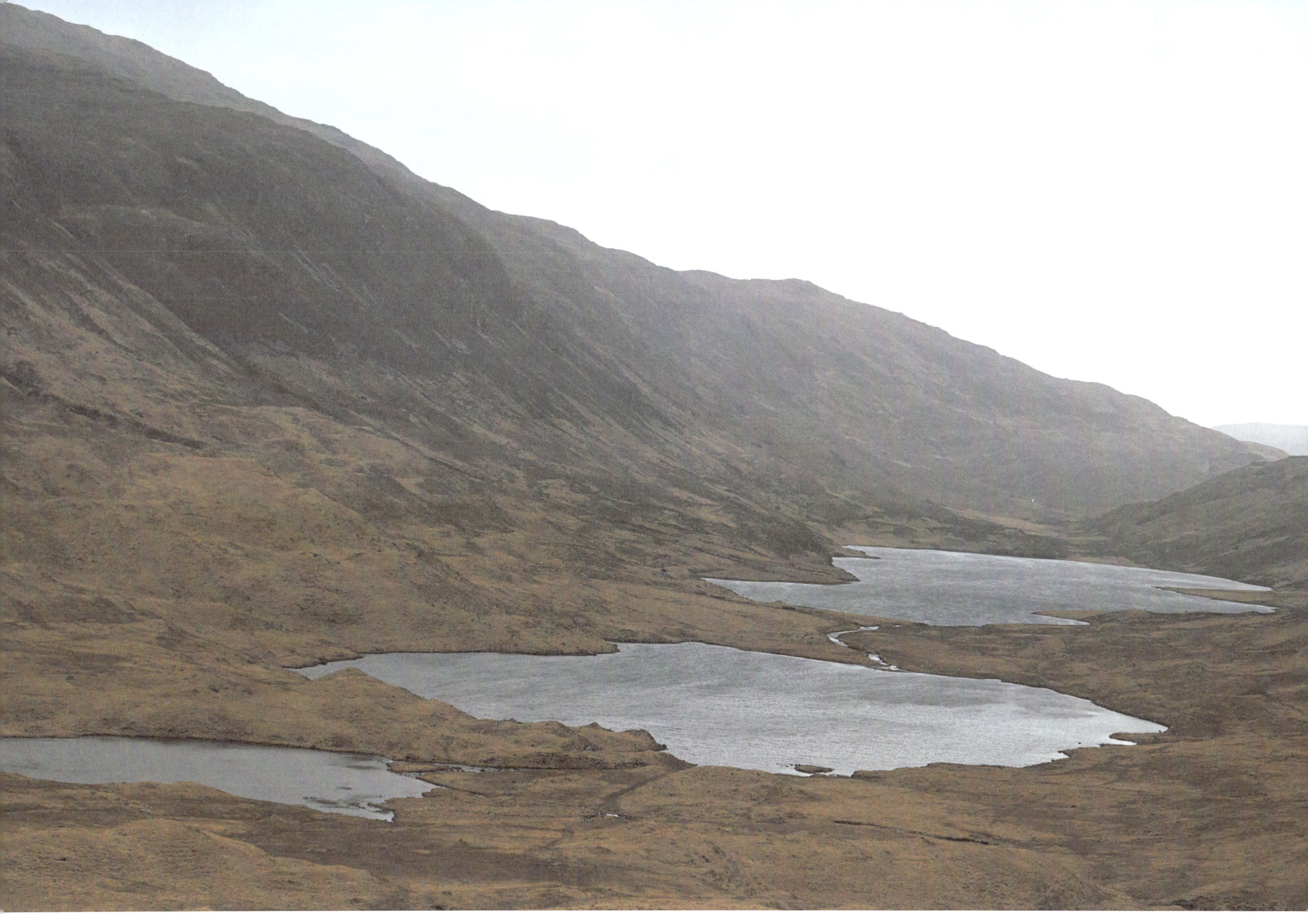

A valley with three small lochs, the photograph was taken from the road close to Ishriff.

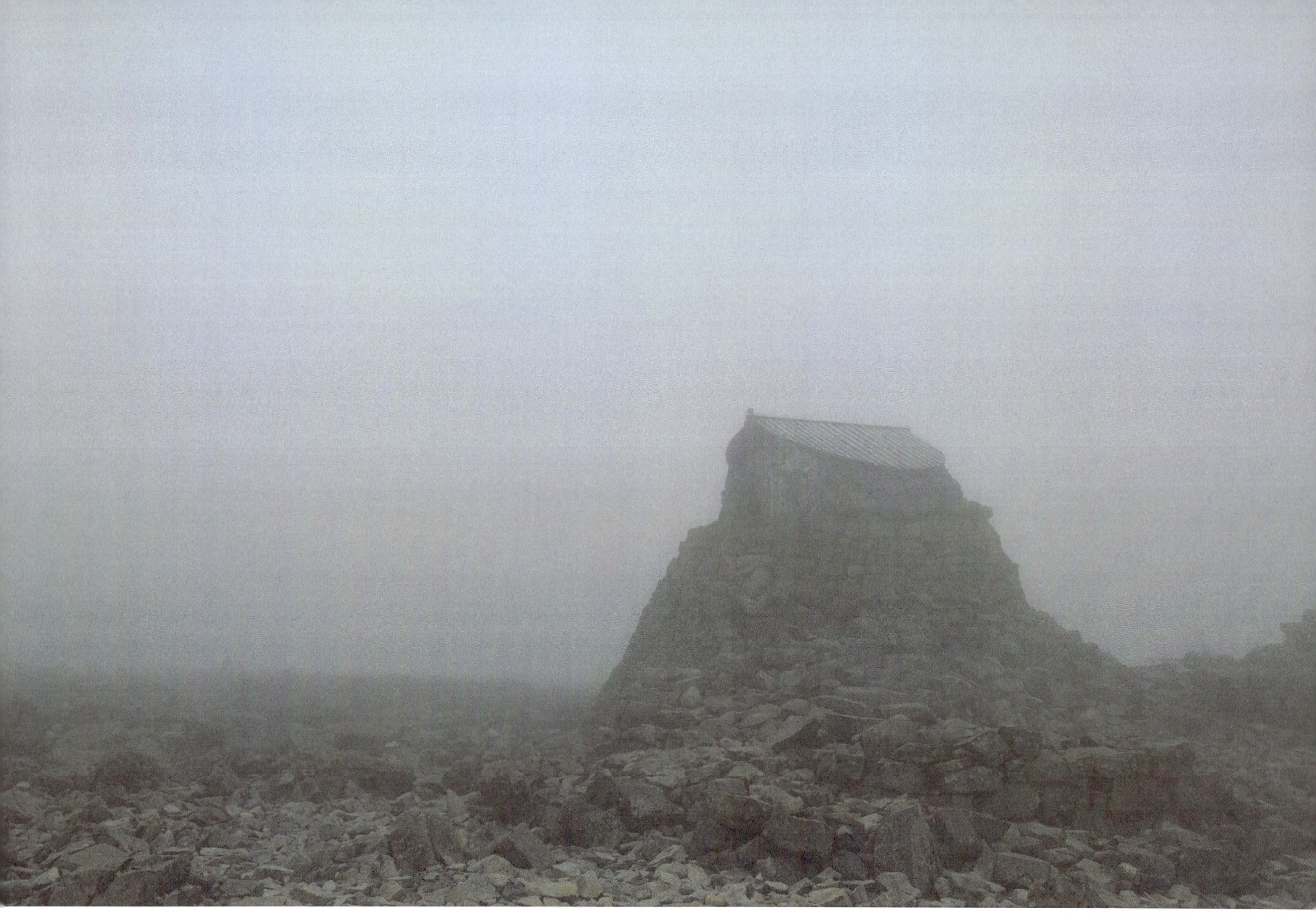

This solid cairn sits at the summit of Ben Nevis, although it appears to balance on a surface of volcanic rock.

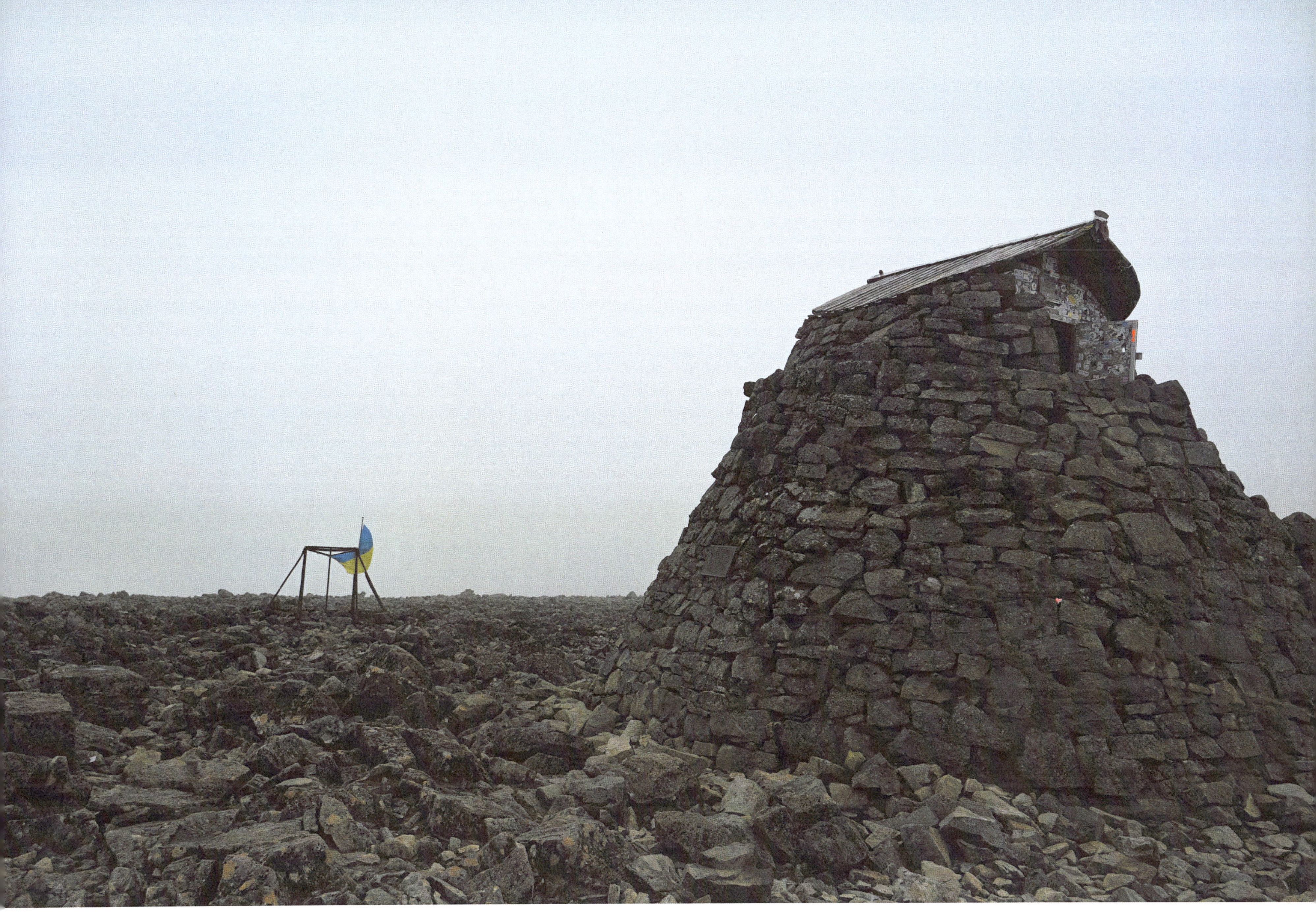

The mist clears and the Ukrainian flag flutters against a backdrop as desolate as the moon.

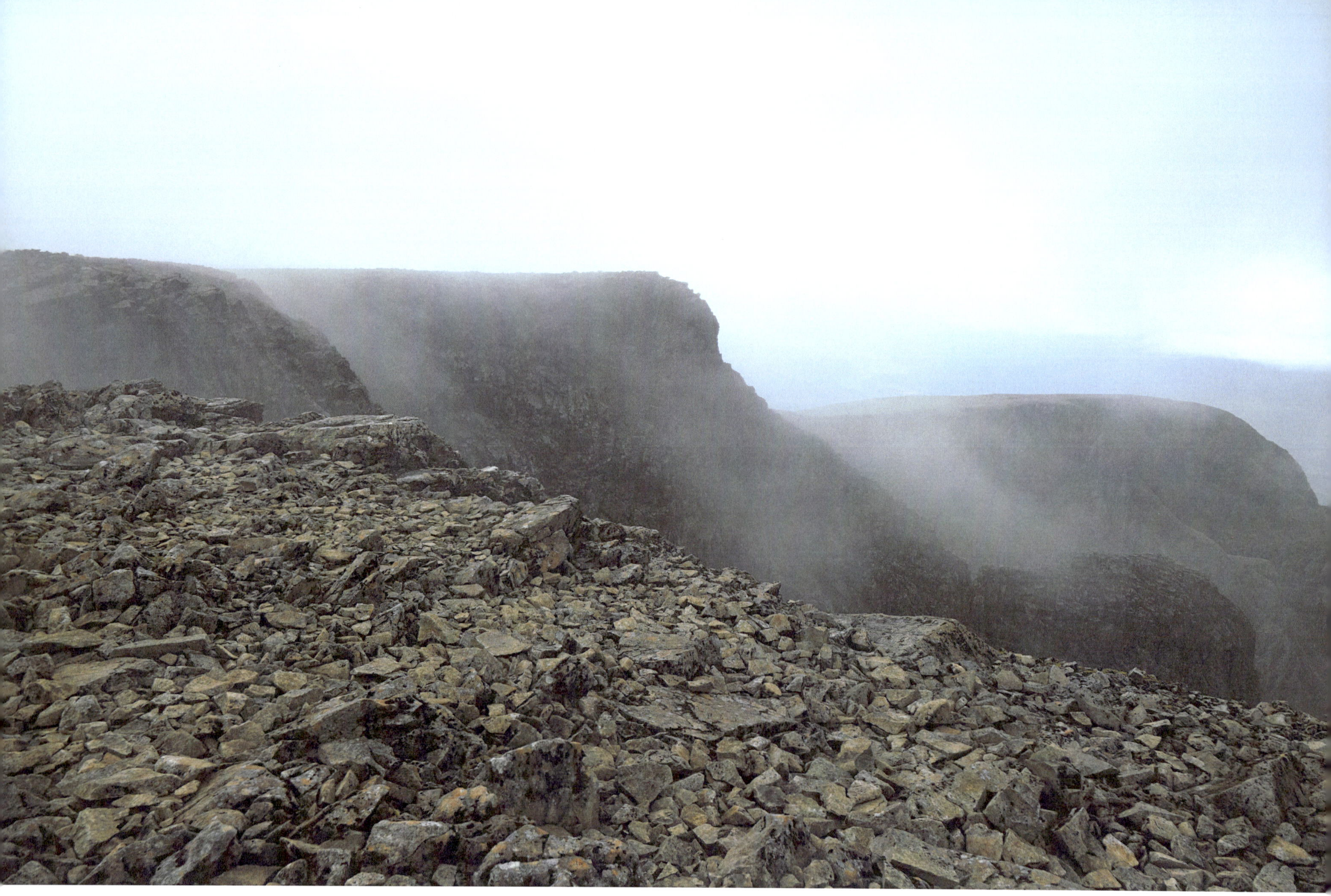

The mist floats like dust from a volcano. The name Ben Nevis is Scottish Gaelic, *beinn* means mountain and *nibheis* translates as venomous or malicious. The oldest climber was in his eighties, so perhaps there is hope for me yet!

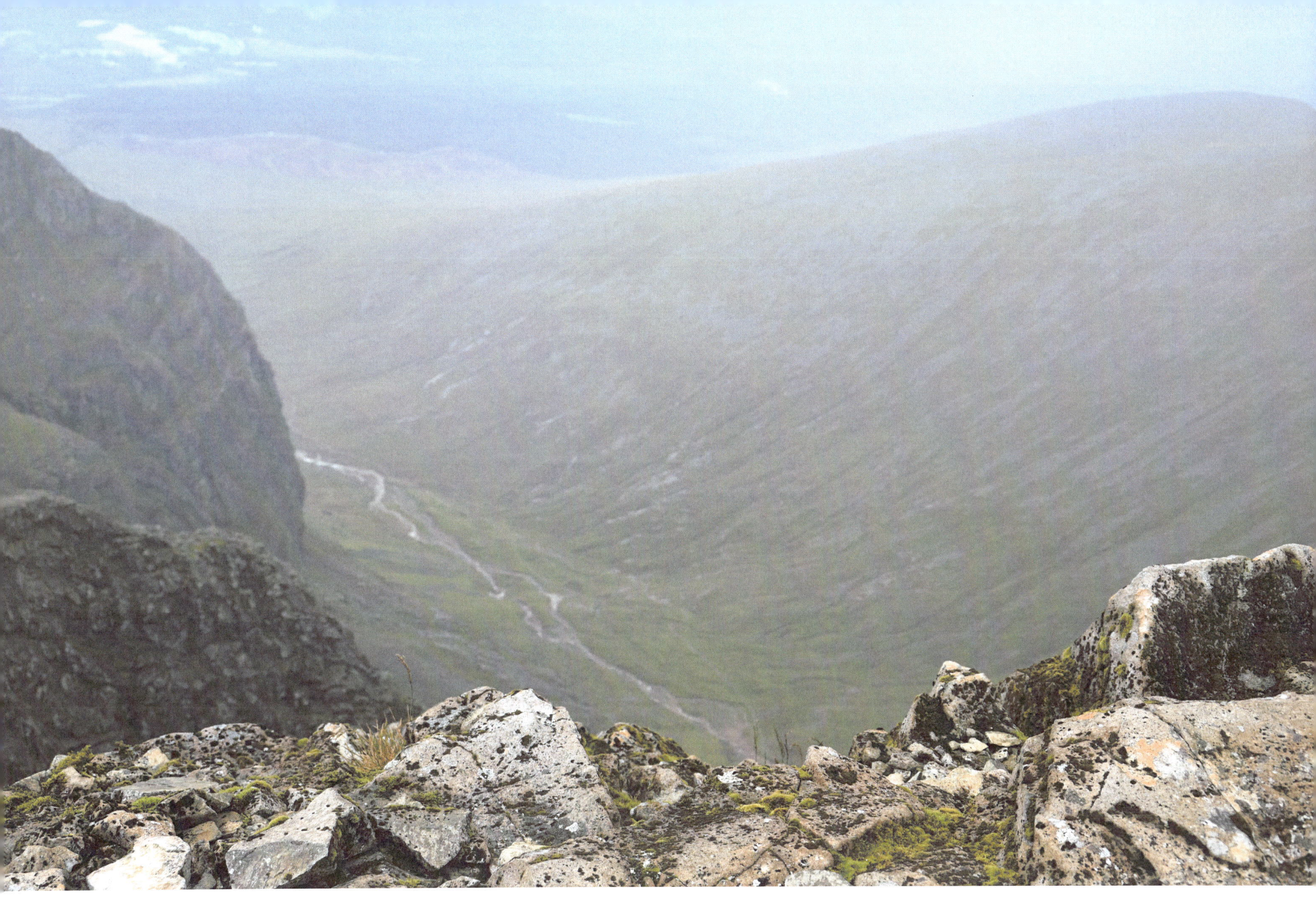

The velvet, green folds of the valley, formed when volcanoes sank to form calderas.

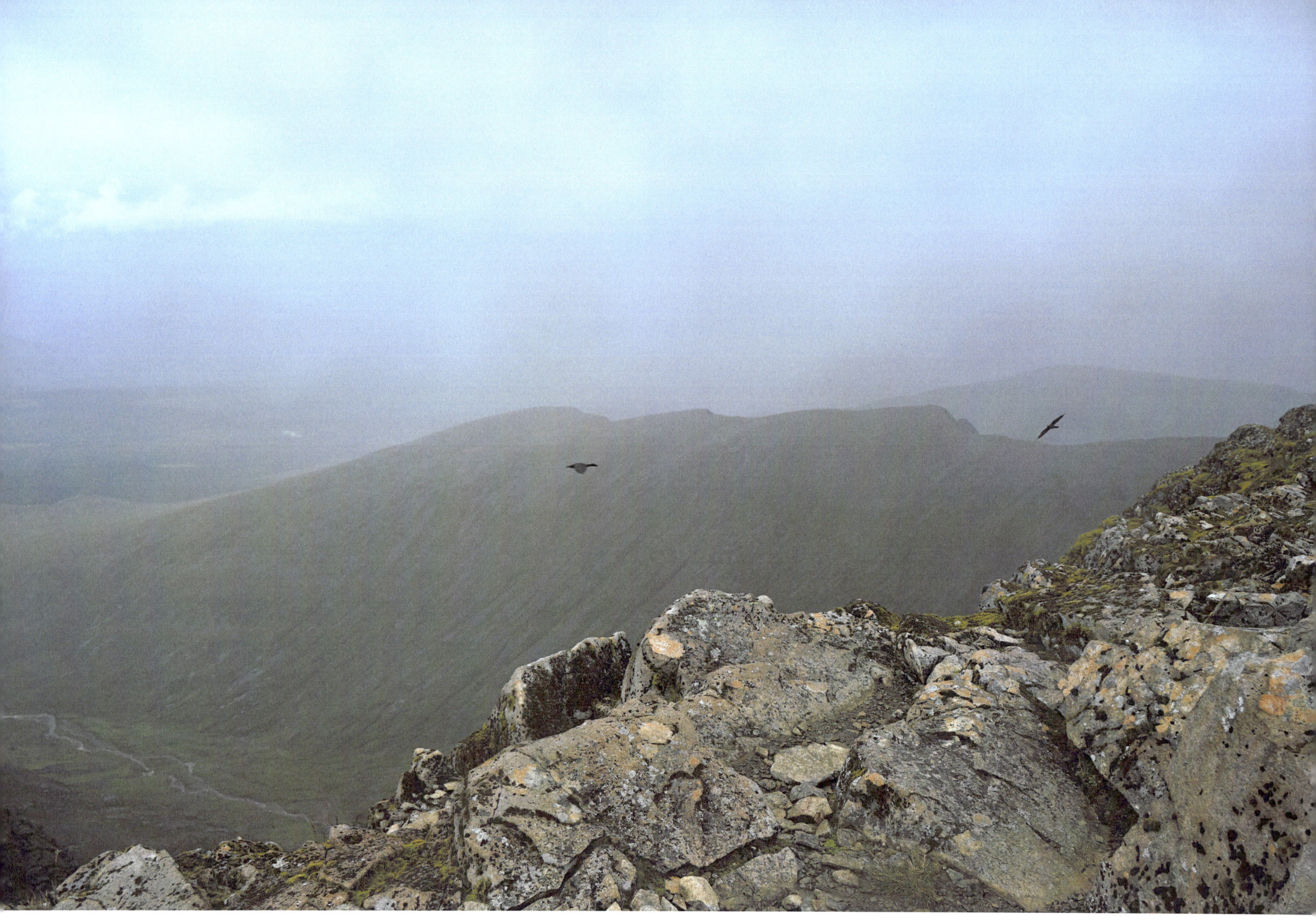

Buzzards break the silence with their calls.

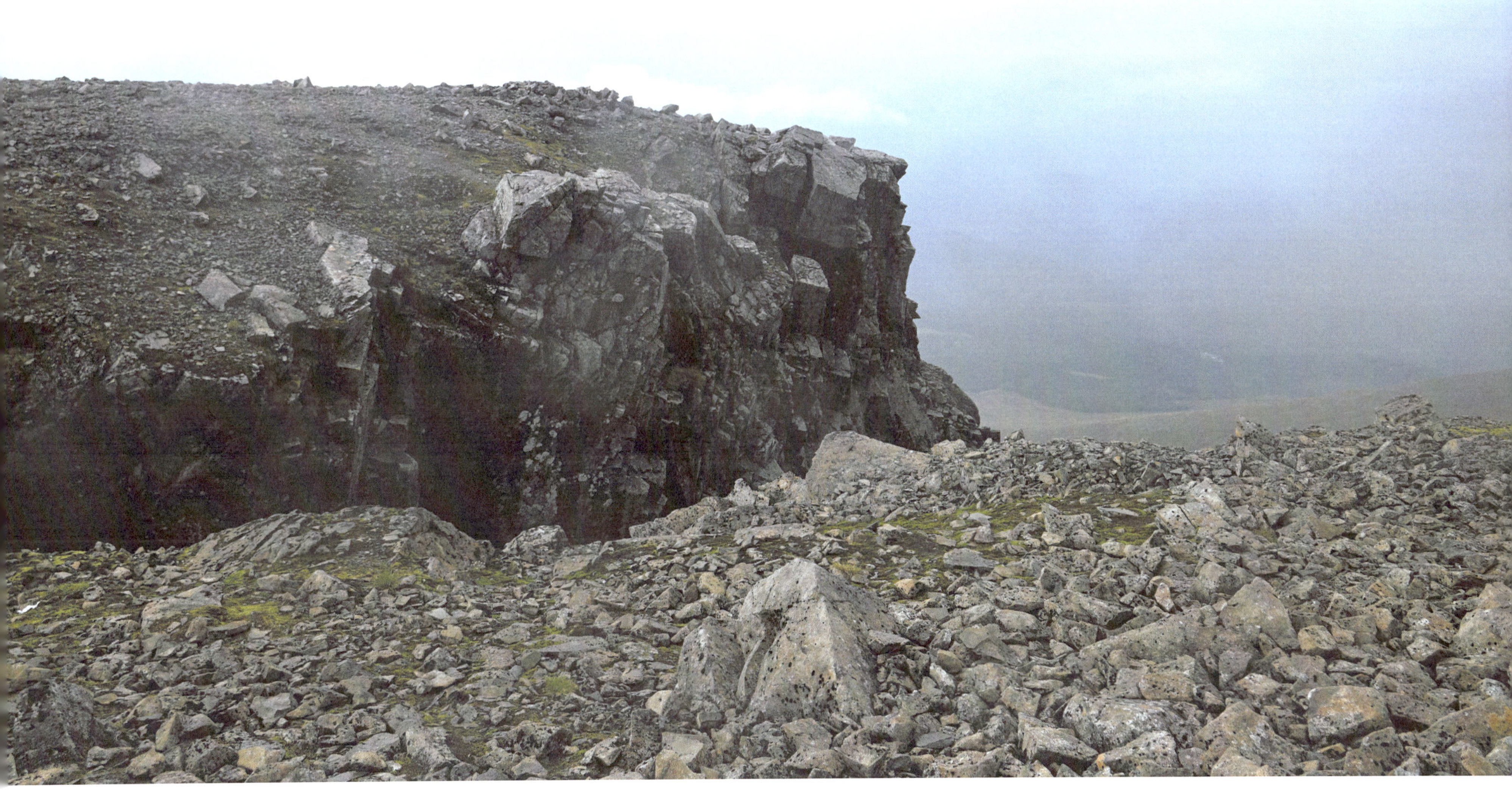

Large shards of volcanic rock make it easy to lose your footing, even in the summer!

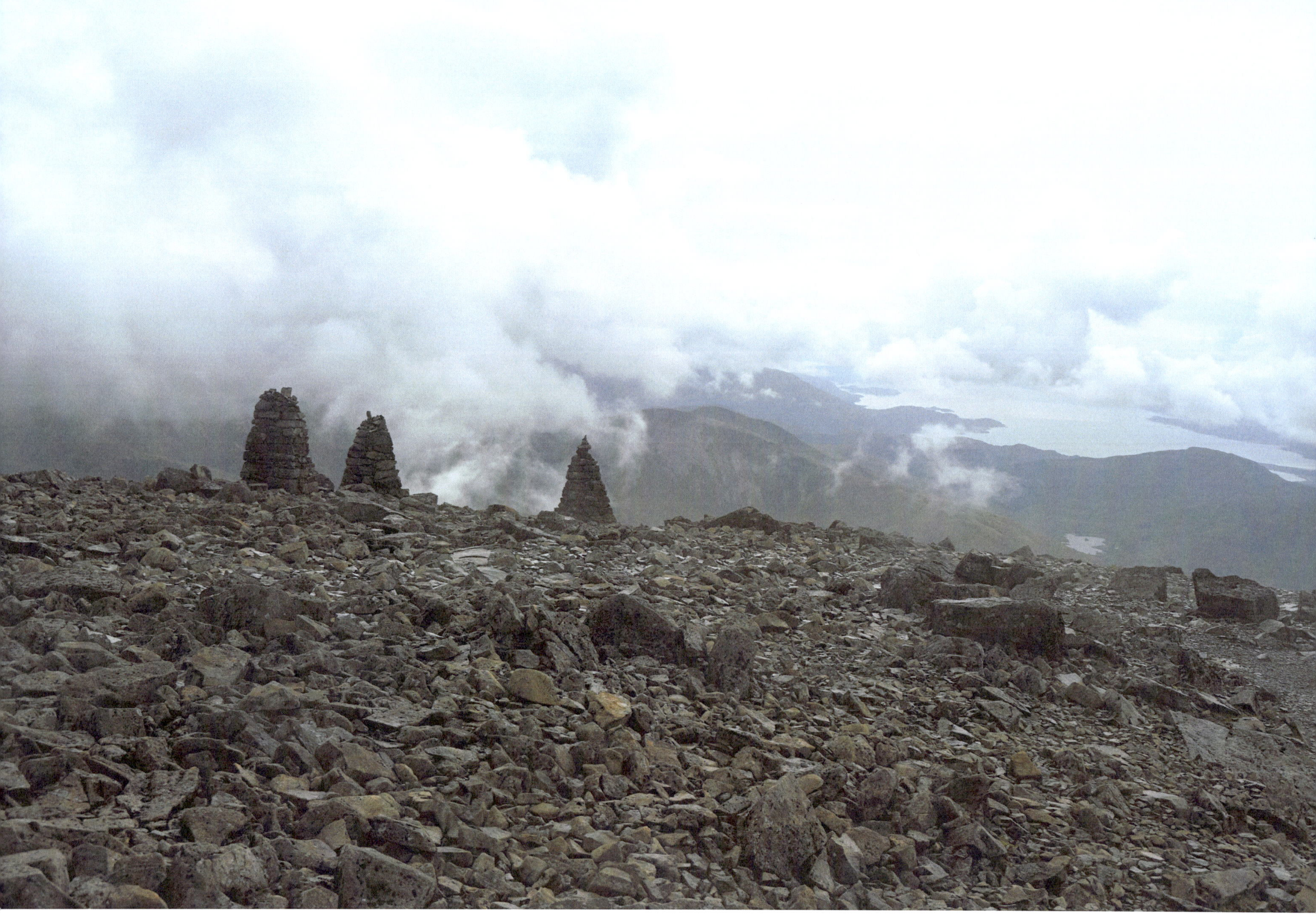

These small cones are built by visitors to the mountain.

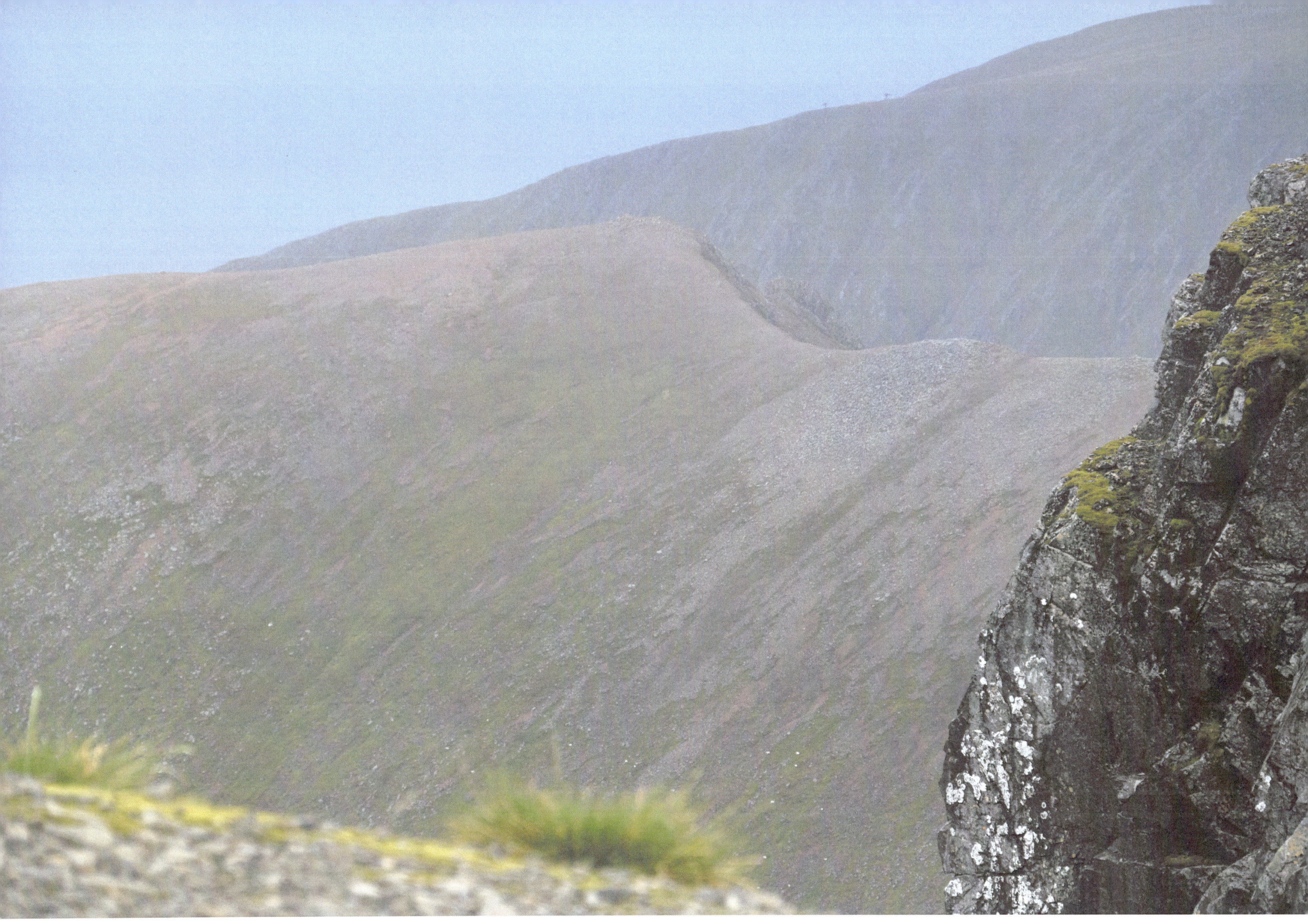

Mid-morning sunlight infuses the mountain with pastel colour.

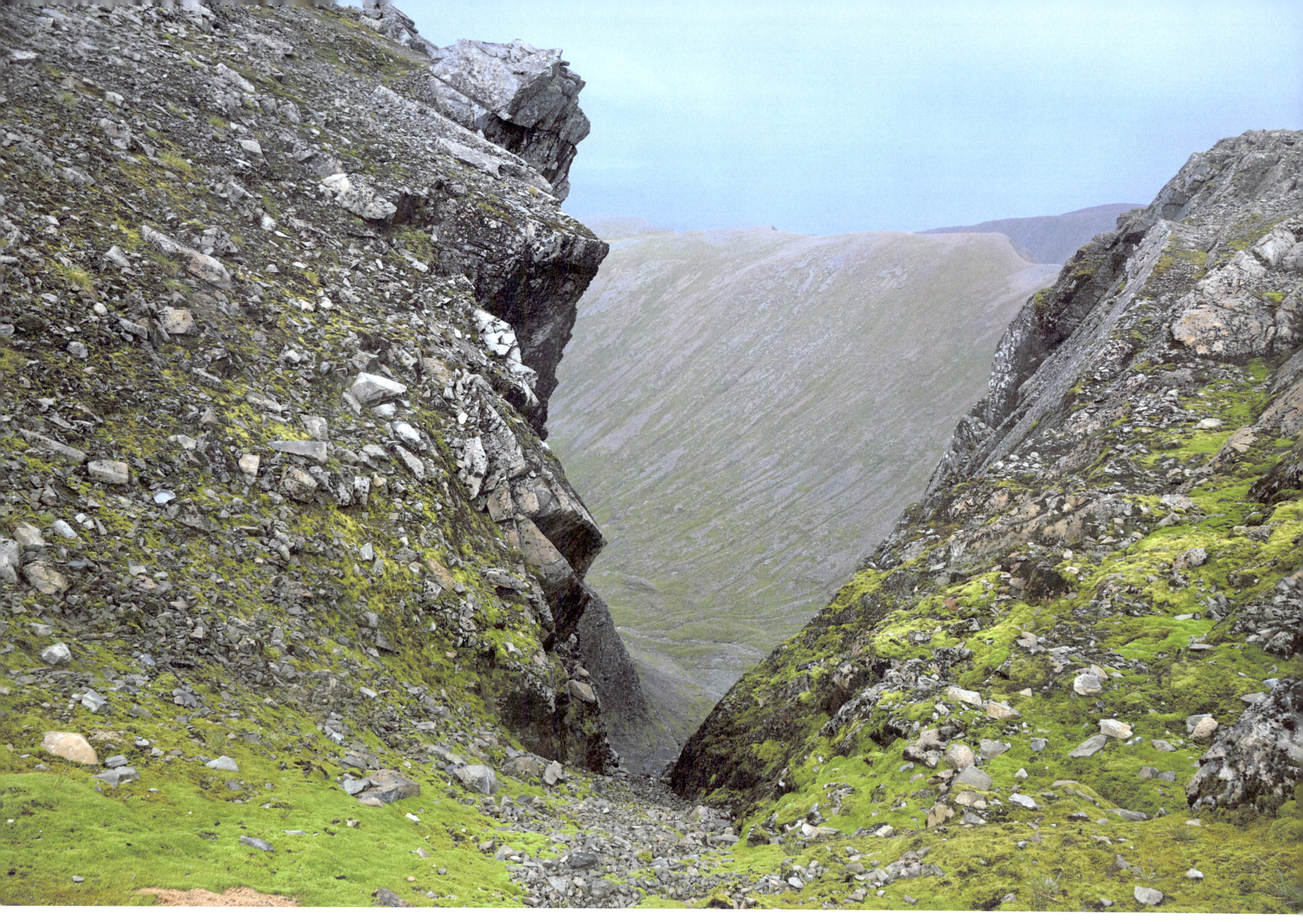

Bright green moss and porella soften the rocks on the lower slopes of the mountain.

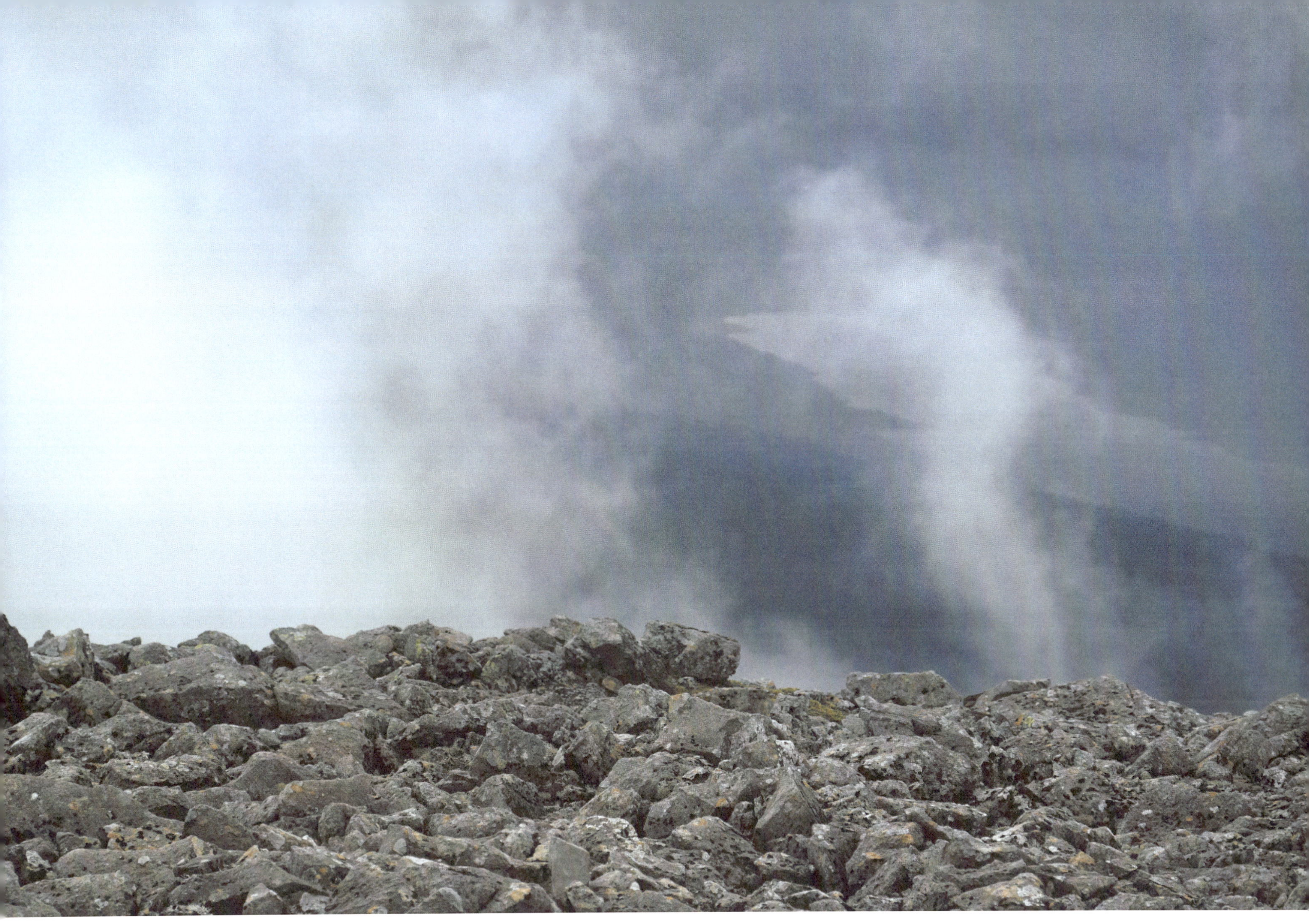

In the distance and through the mist, we can see the loch at last.

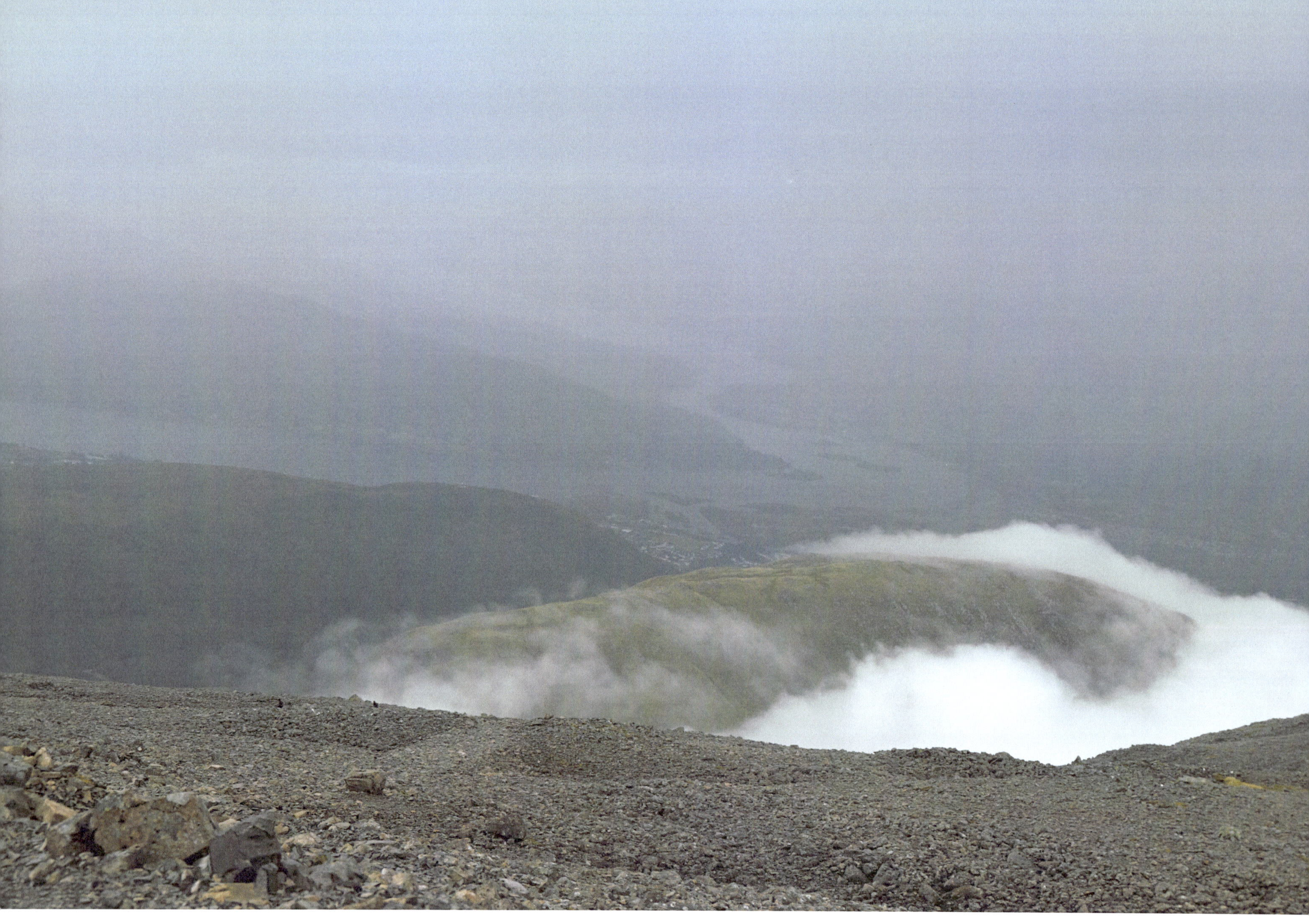

To the Iron Age people of Glen Nevis hill fort, the hill might have resembled a sleeping dragon surrounded by clouds.

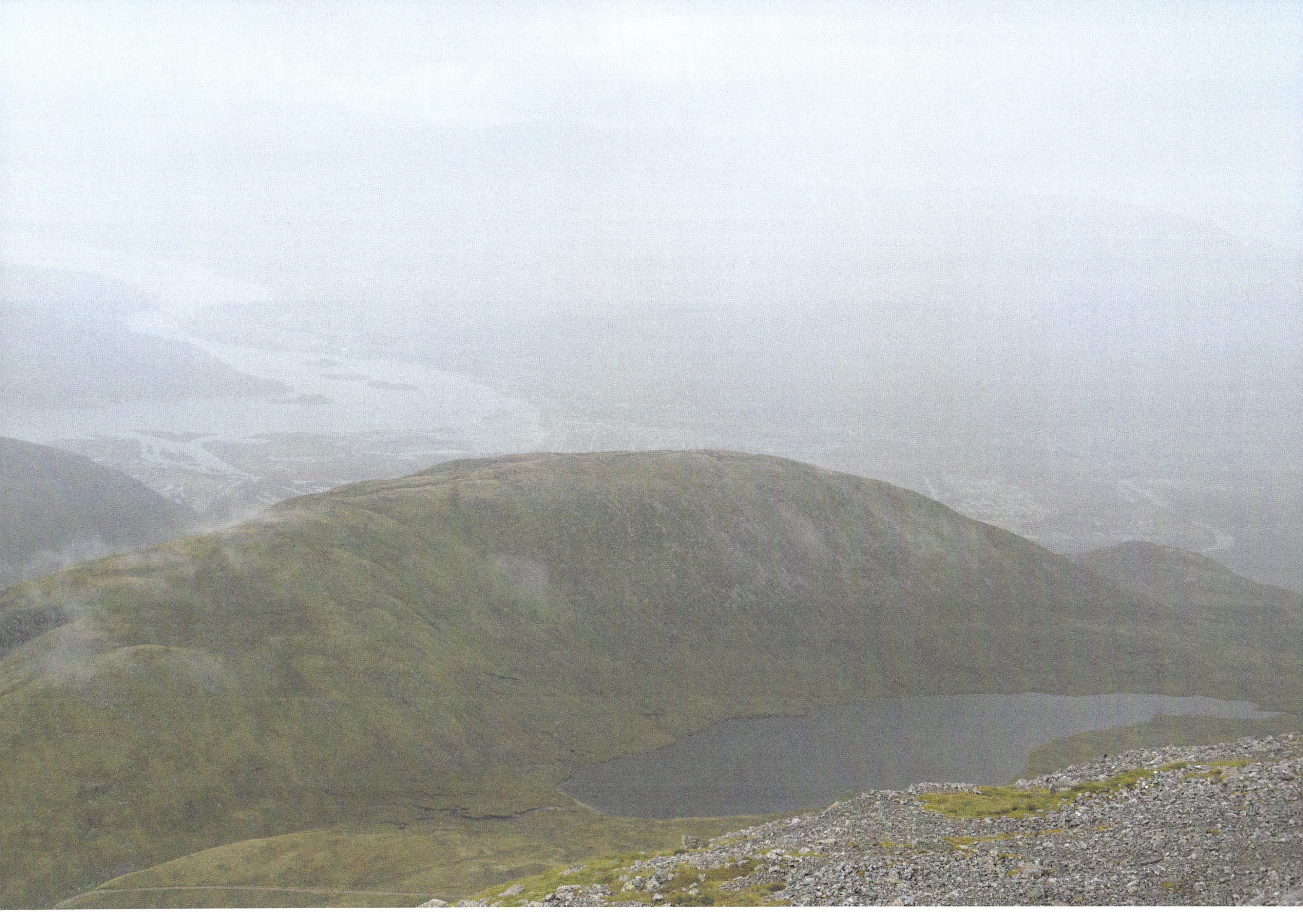

A little loch nestling by the dragon.

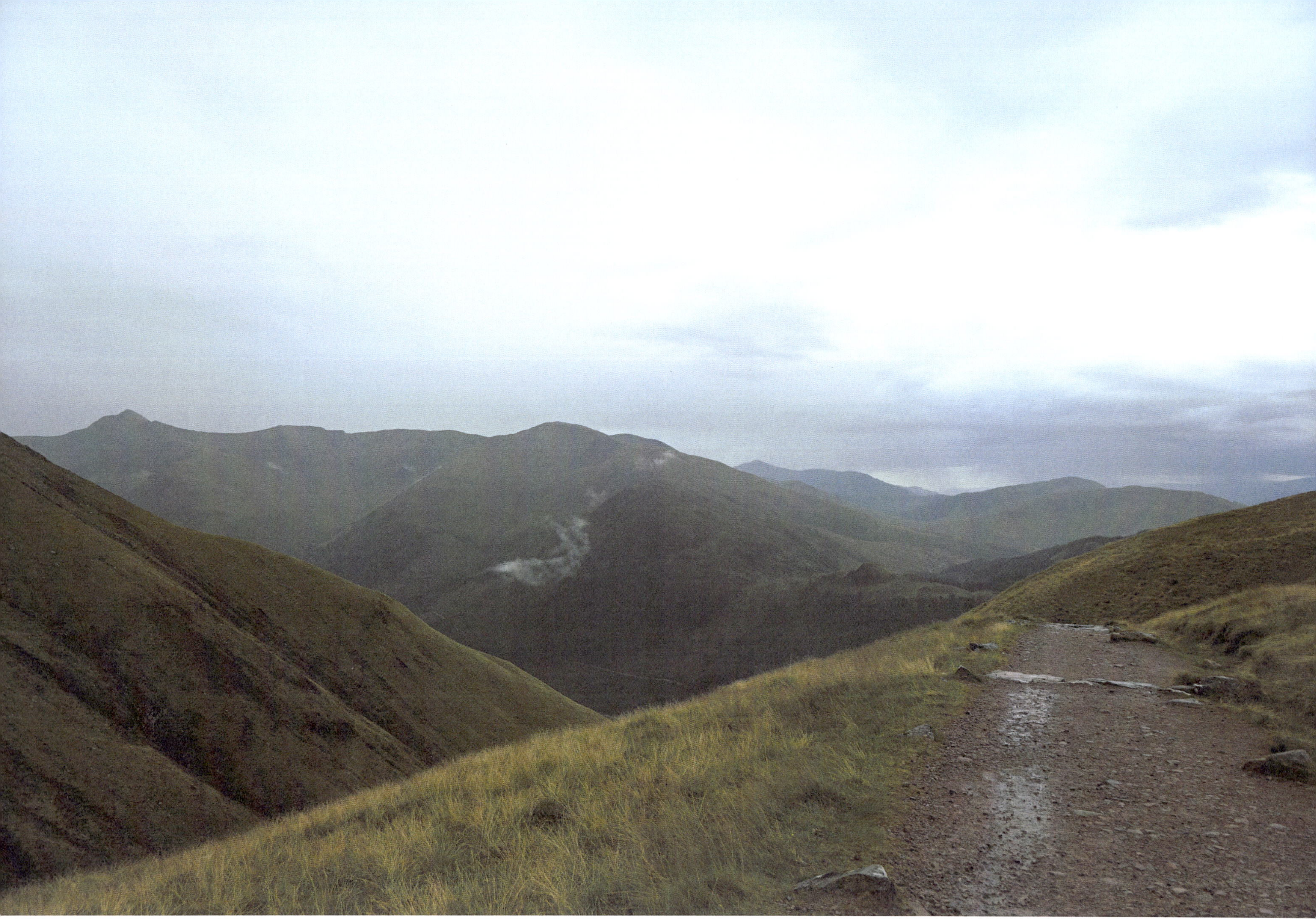

The path leading down from the mountains.

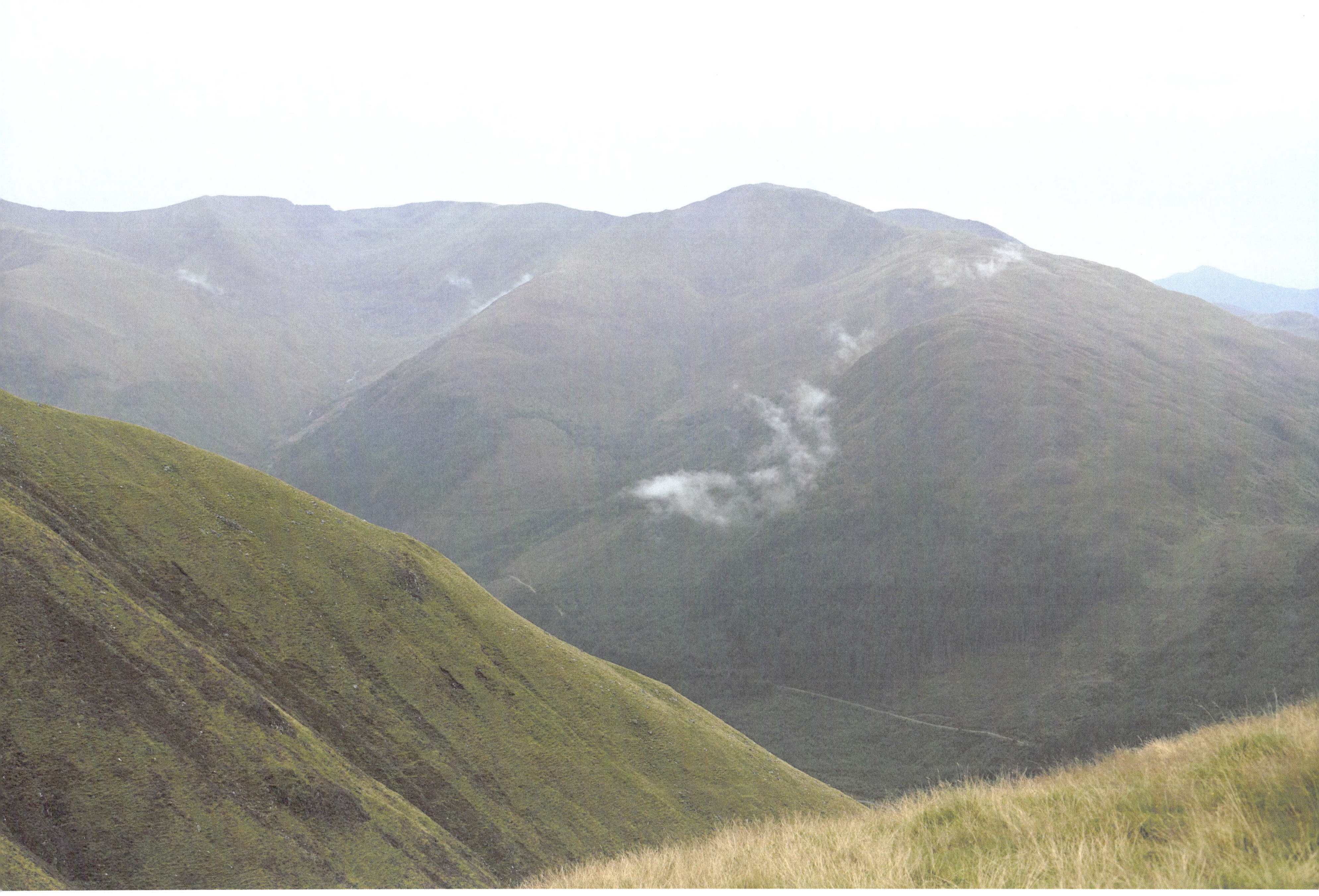

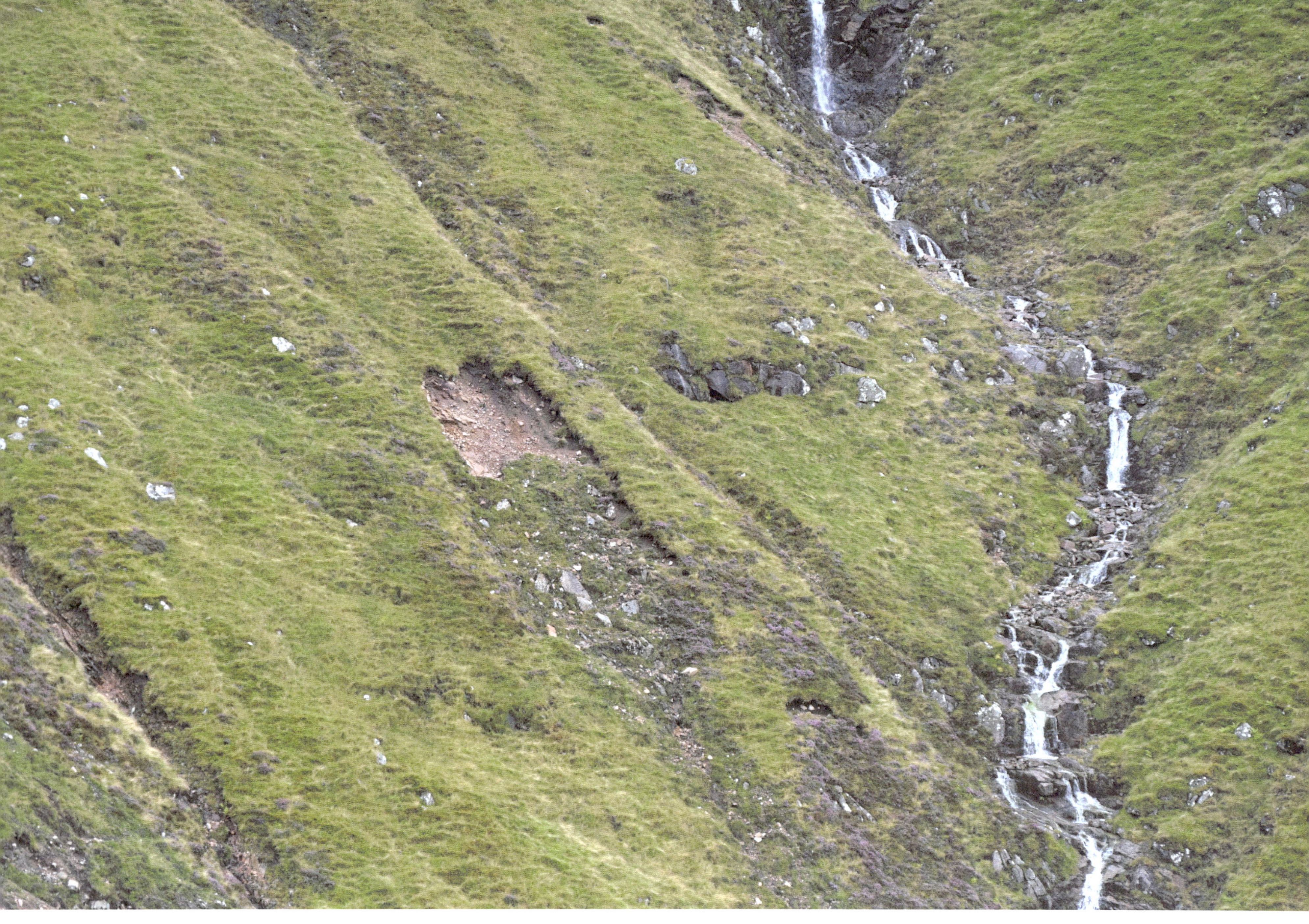

Narrow streams gush over the rock beds.

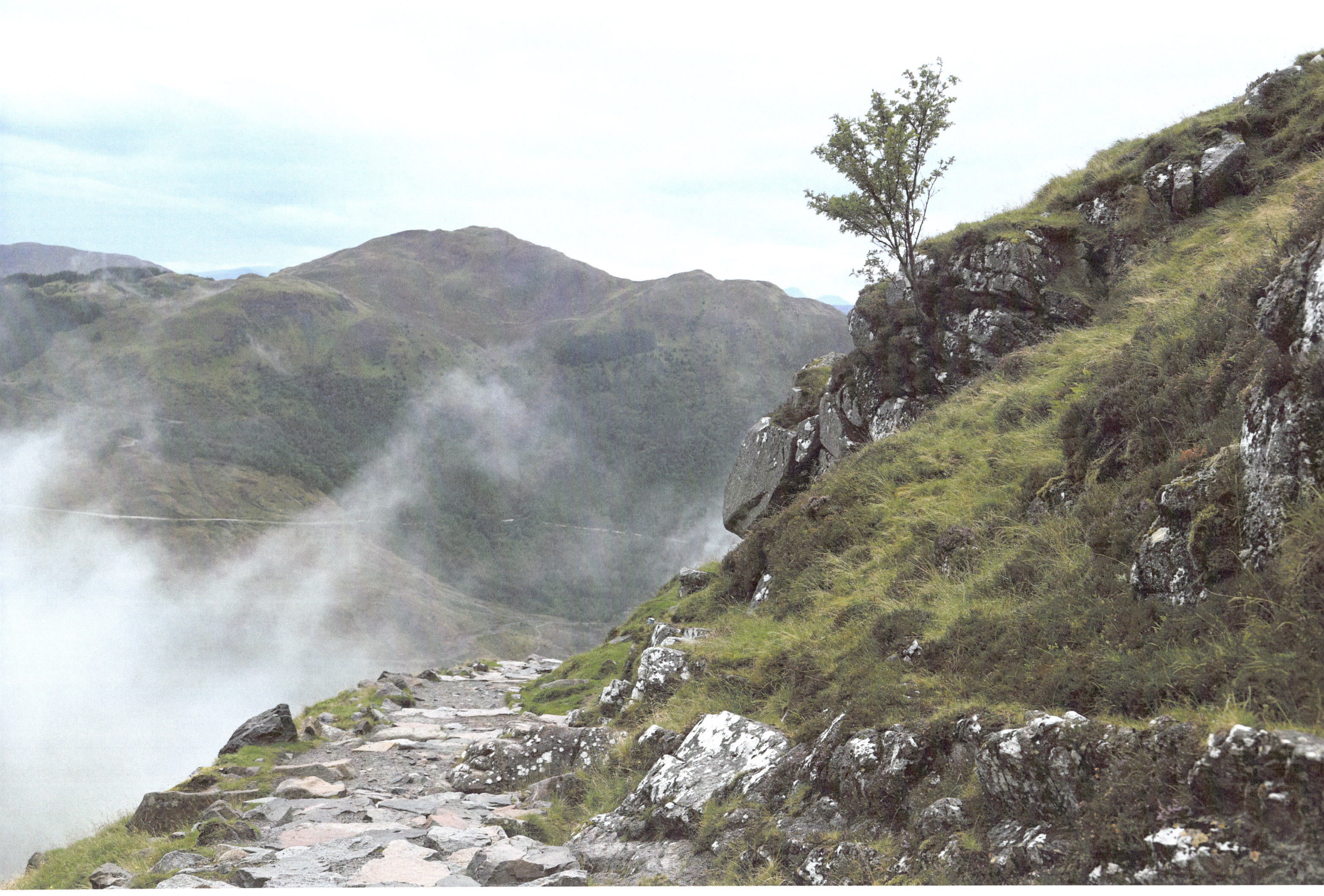

The roots of a small tree cling determinedly to the rocks as the mist rises.

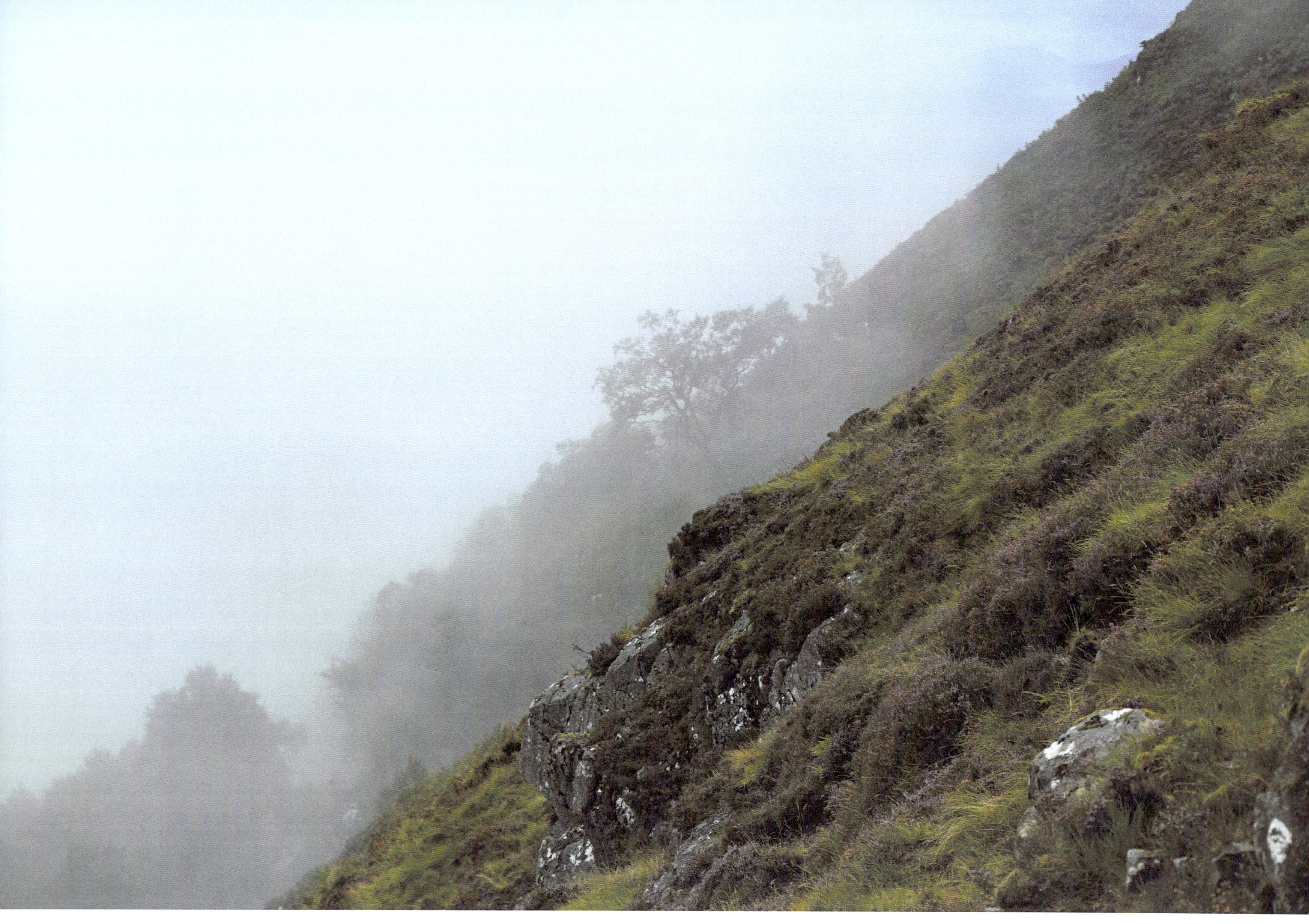

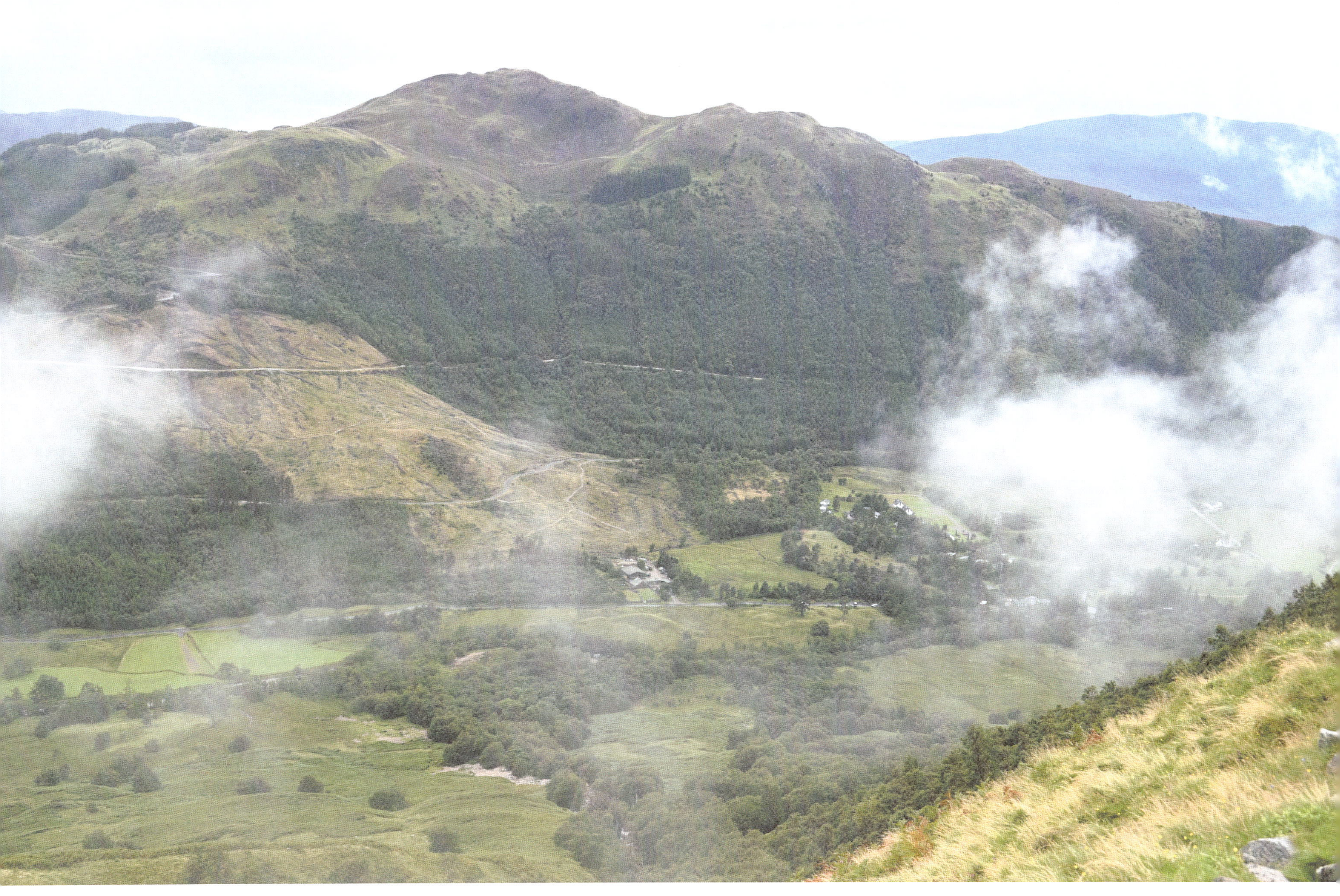

The view as we descend the mountain along a woodland path.

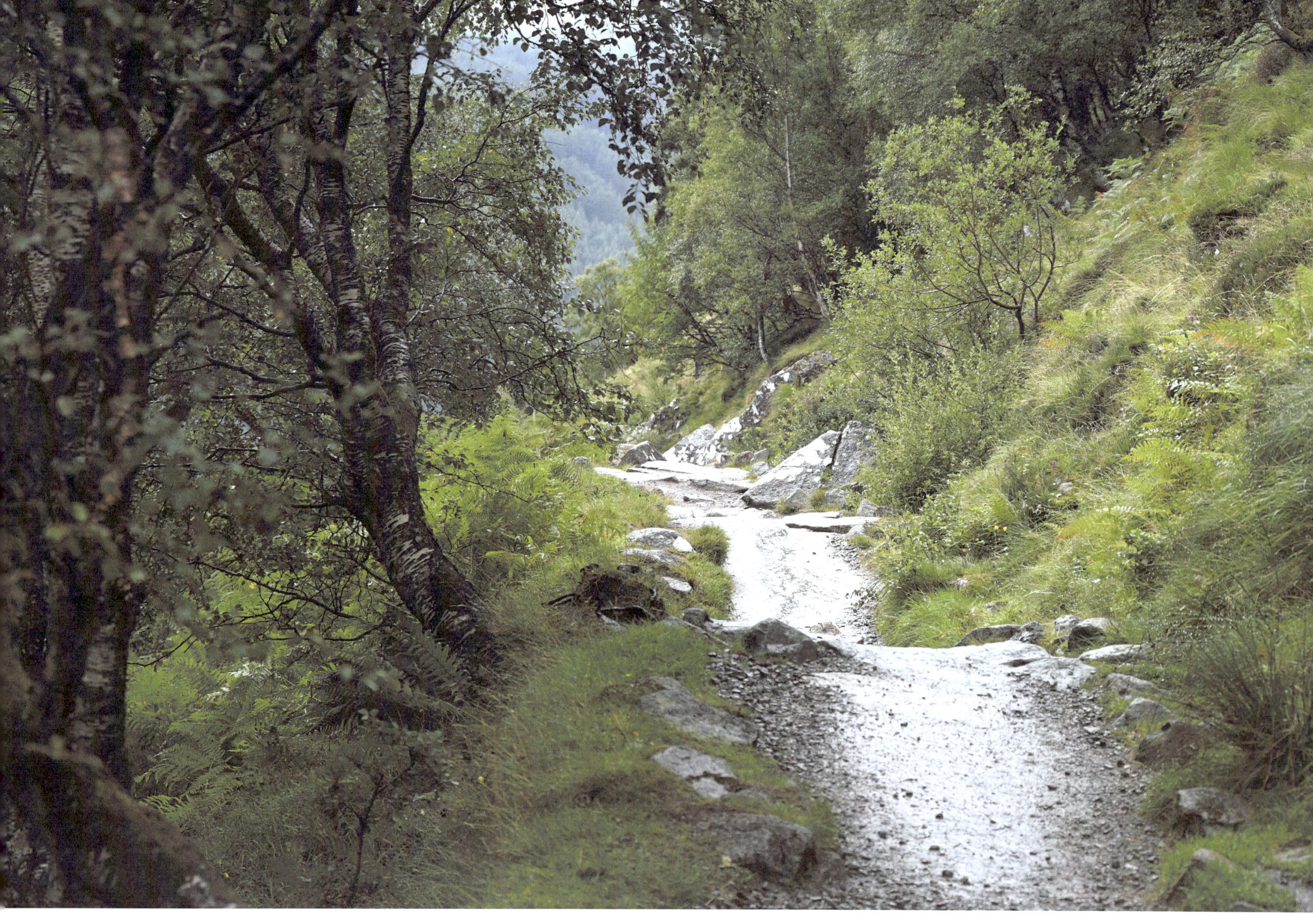

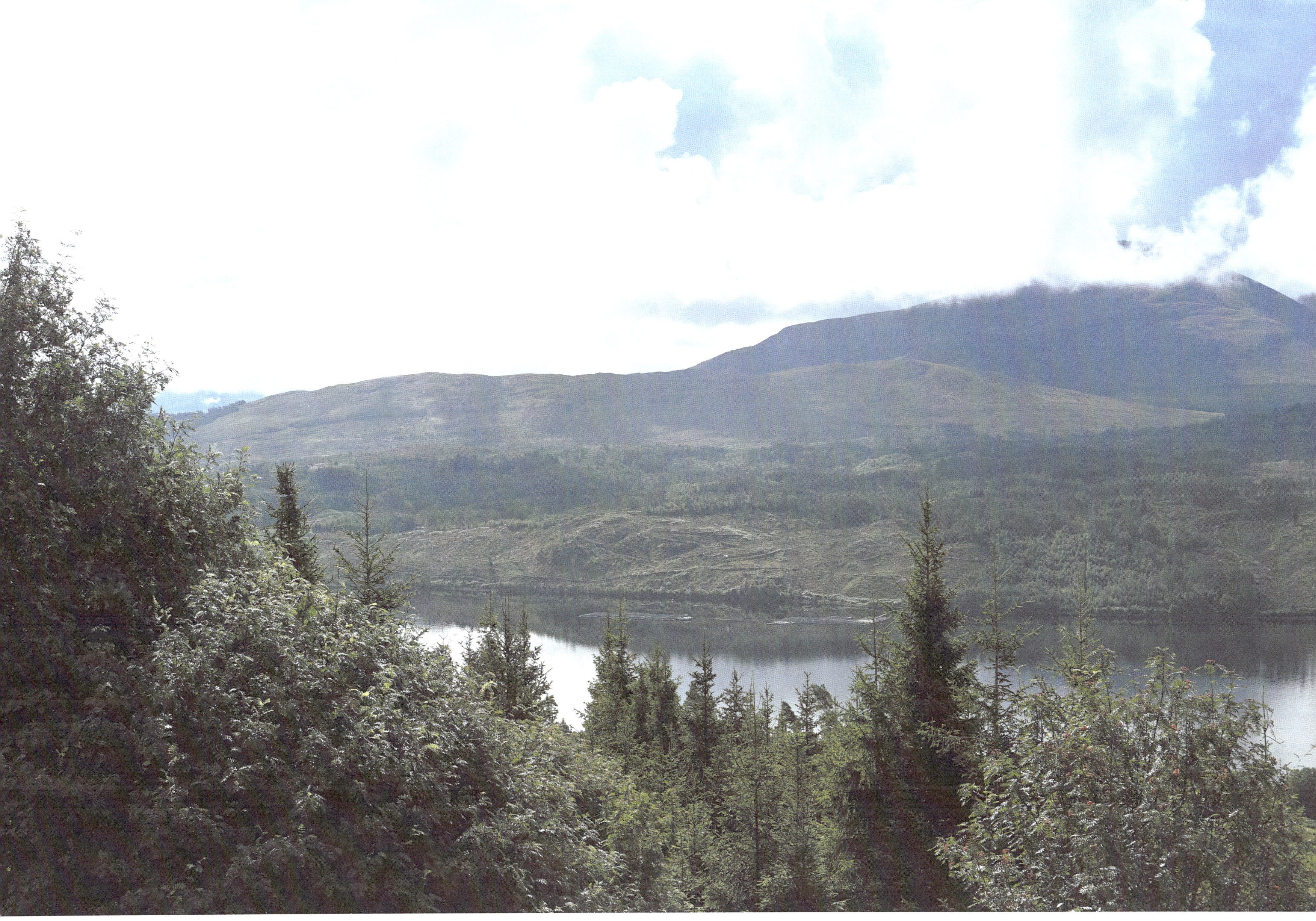

On the road to Skye, the lochs and mountains beckon us on.

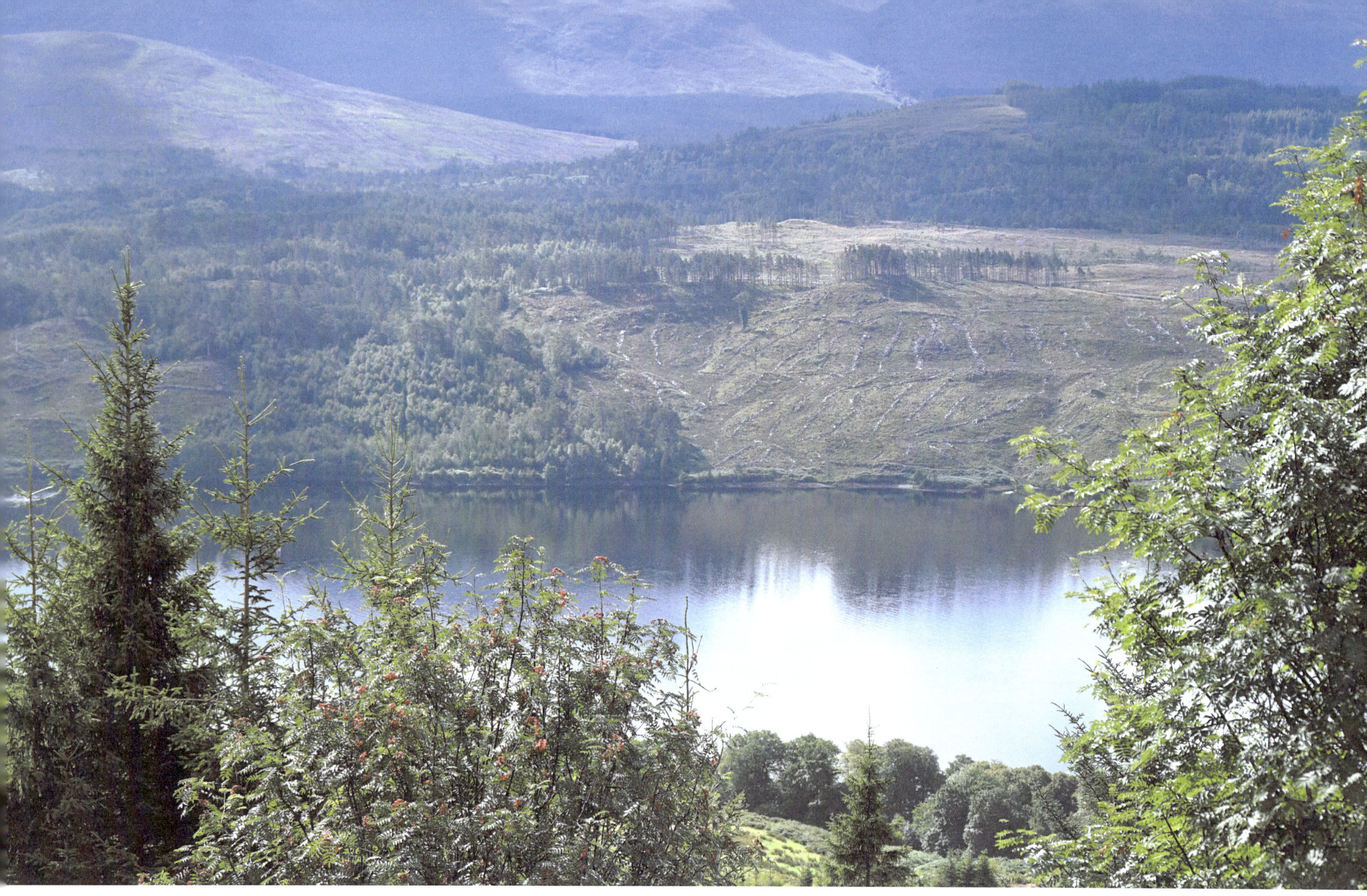

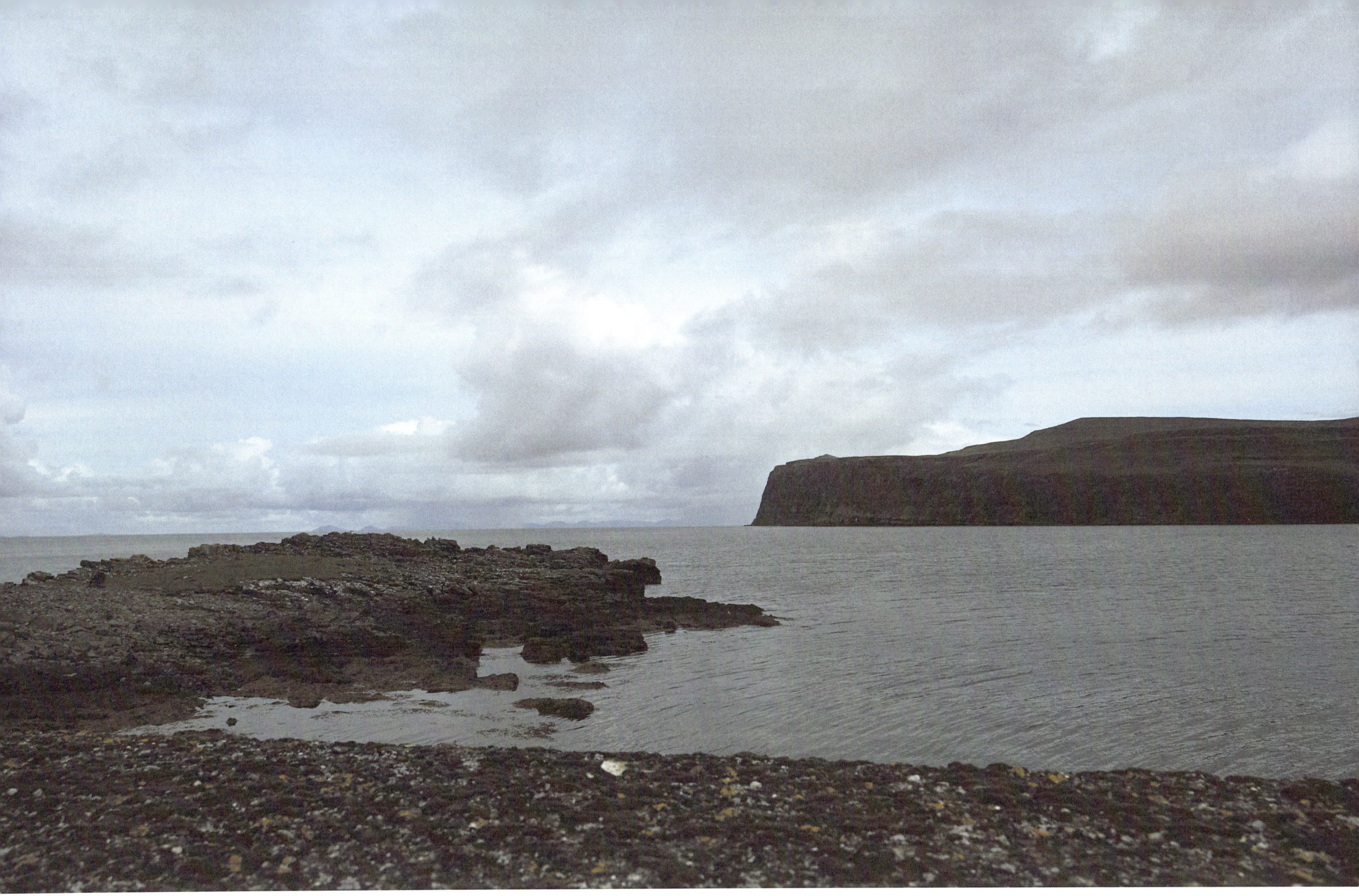

We leave Glenelg to Kylerhea on Skye after leaving narrow, winding roads through the mountains.
The little harbour is lovely – sleek, fat seals sunbathe upon the rocks. A collie dog helps
the ferryman by trying to untie the moorings with his teeth.

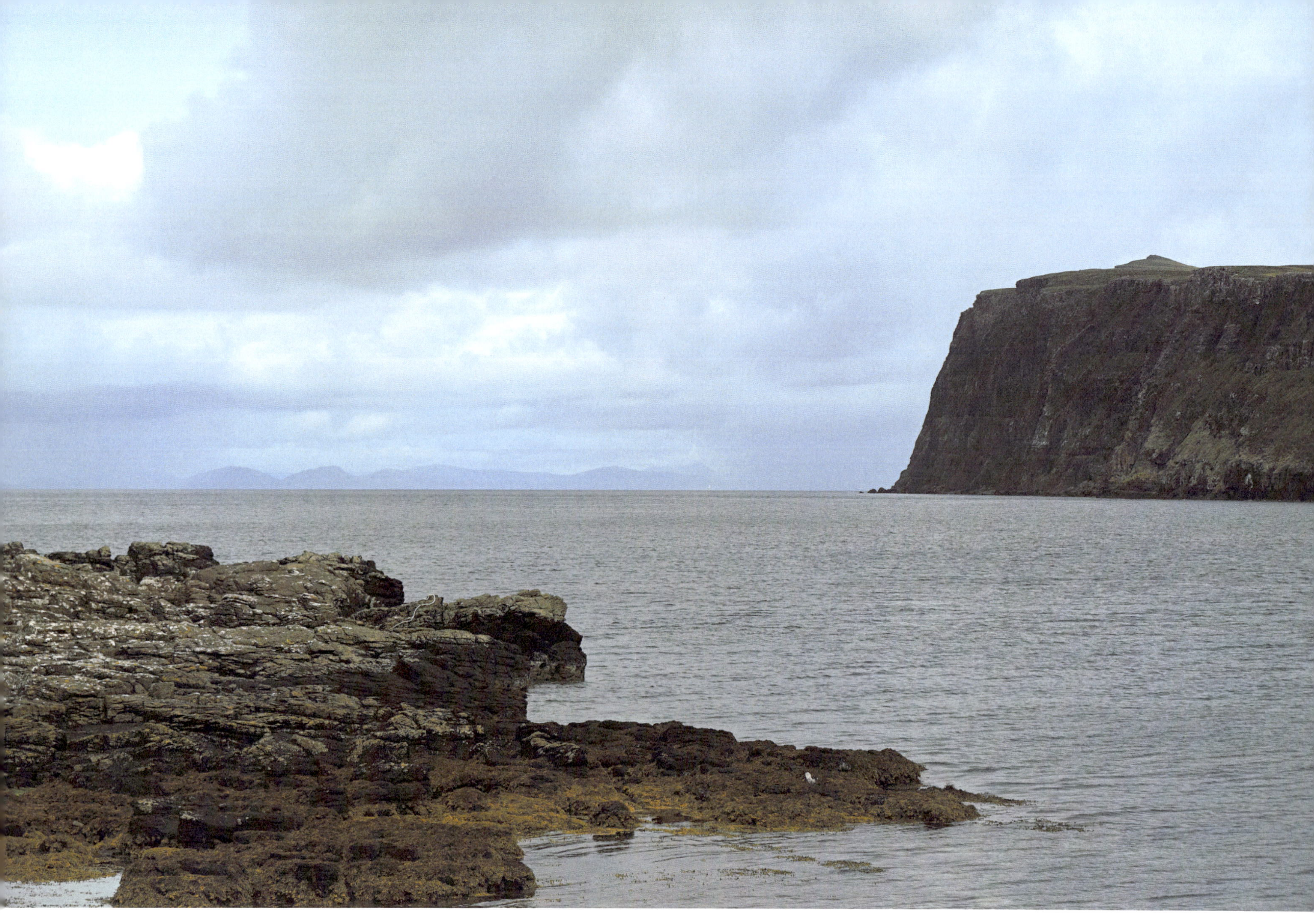

The coastline near Glendale, north-west Skye, the home of the Glendale Martyrs.

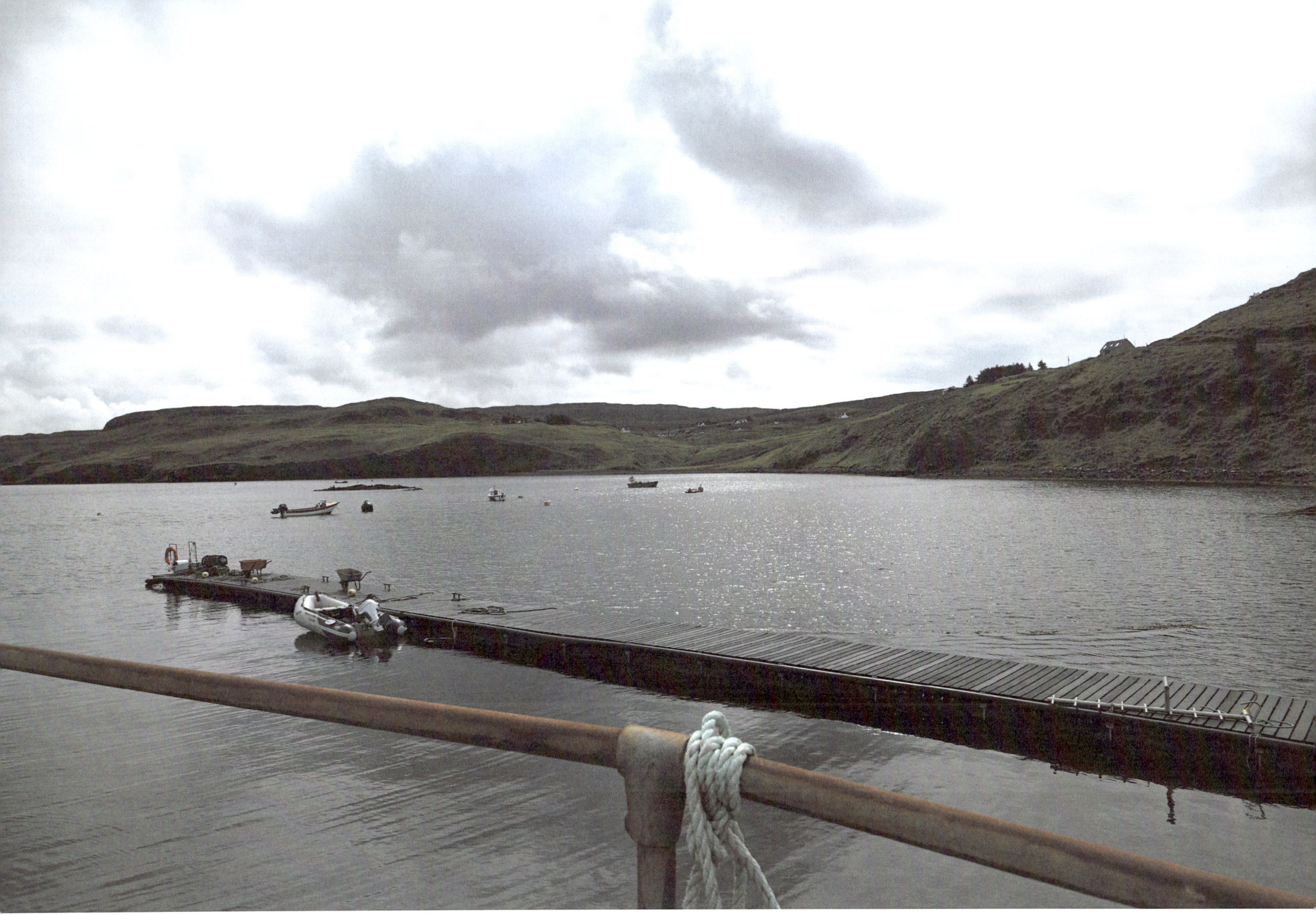

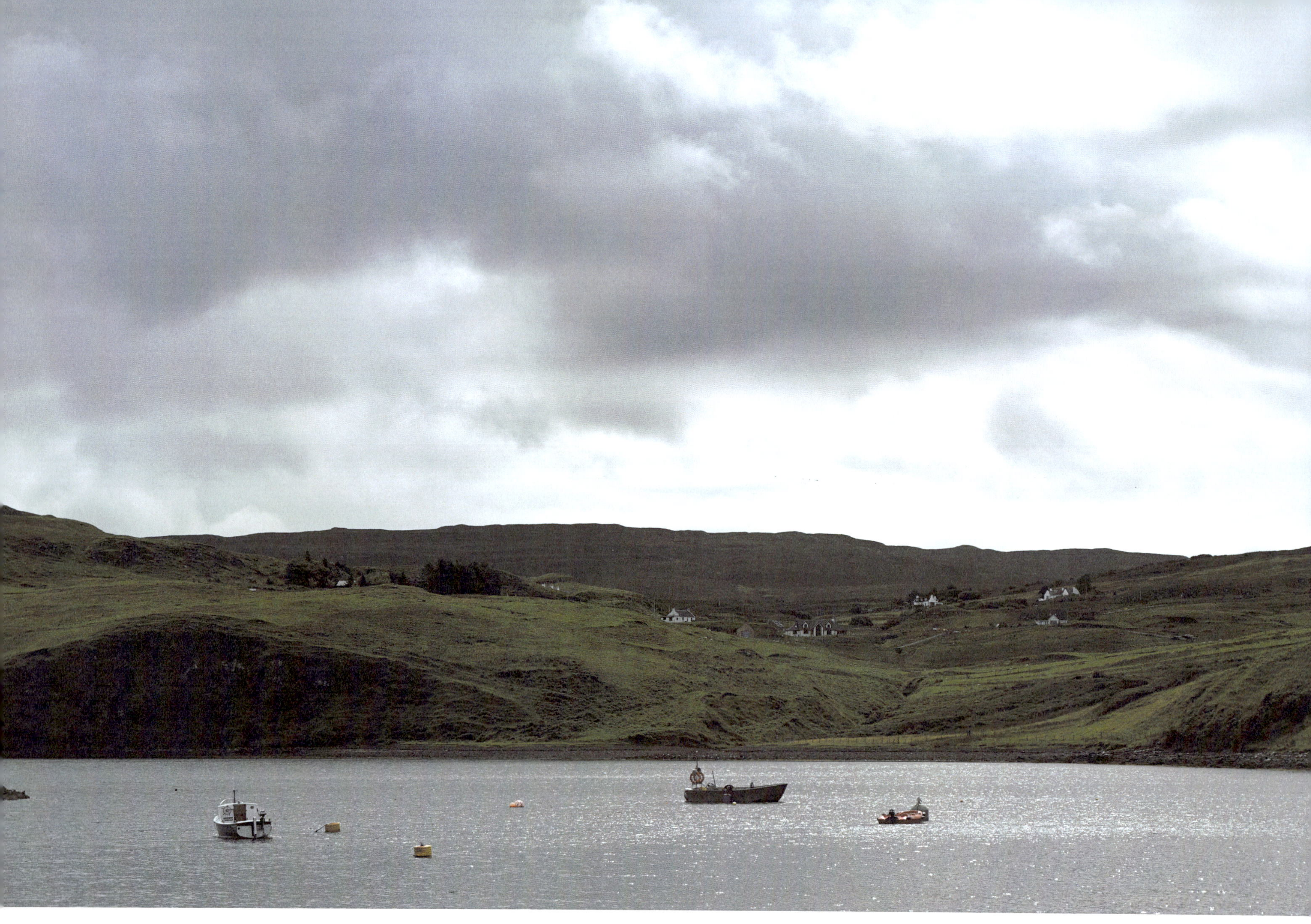

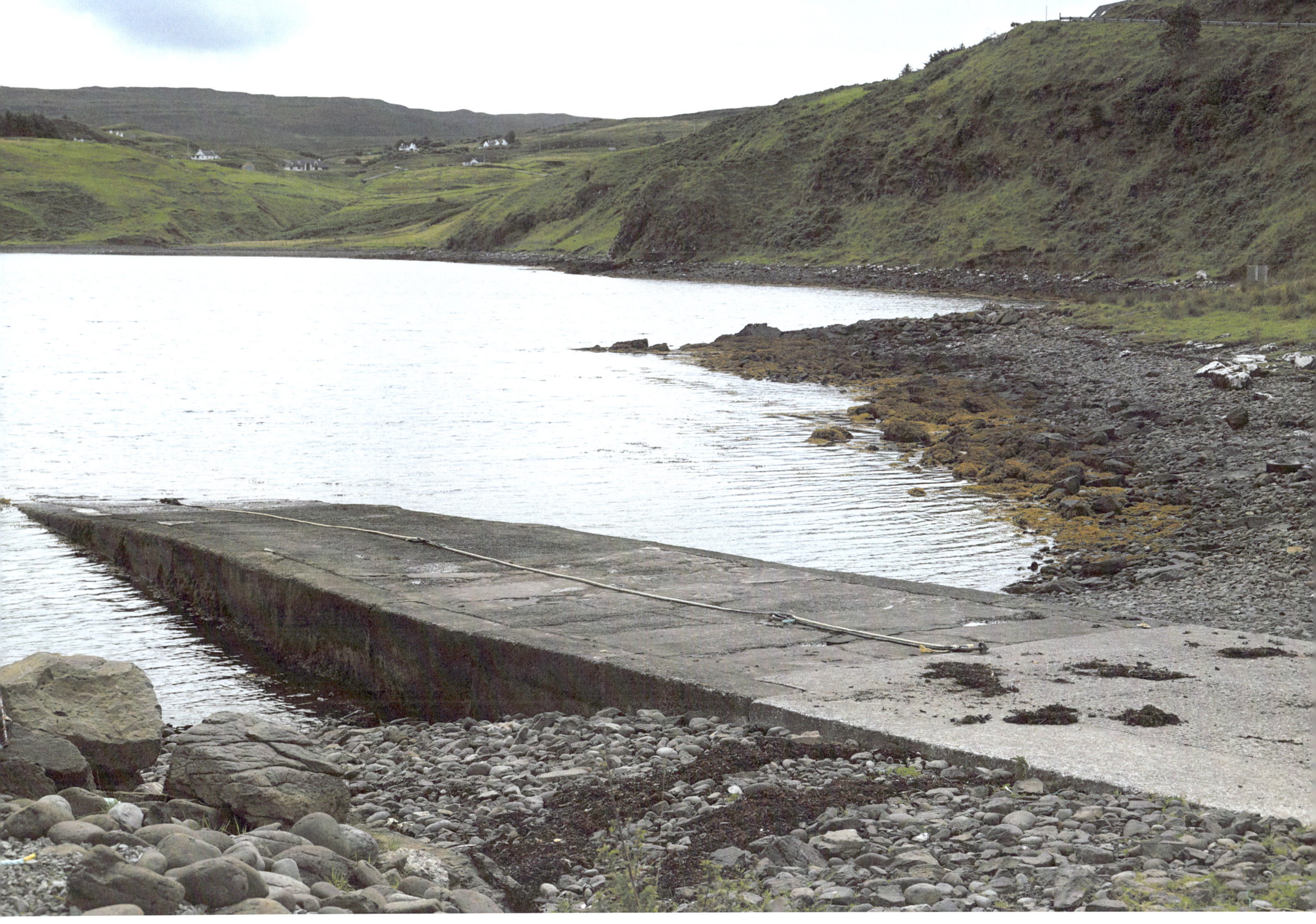

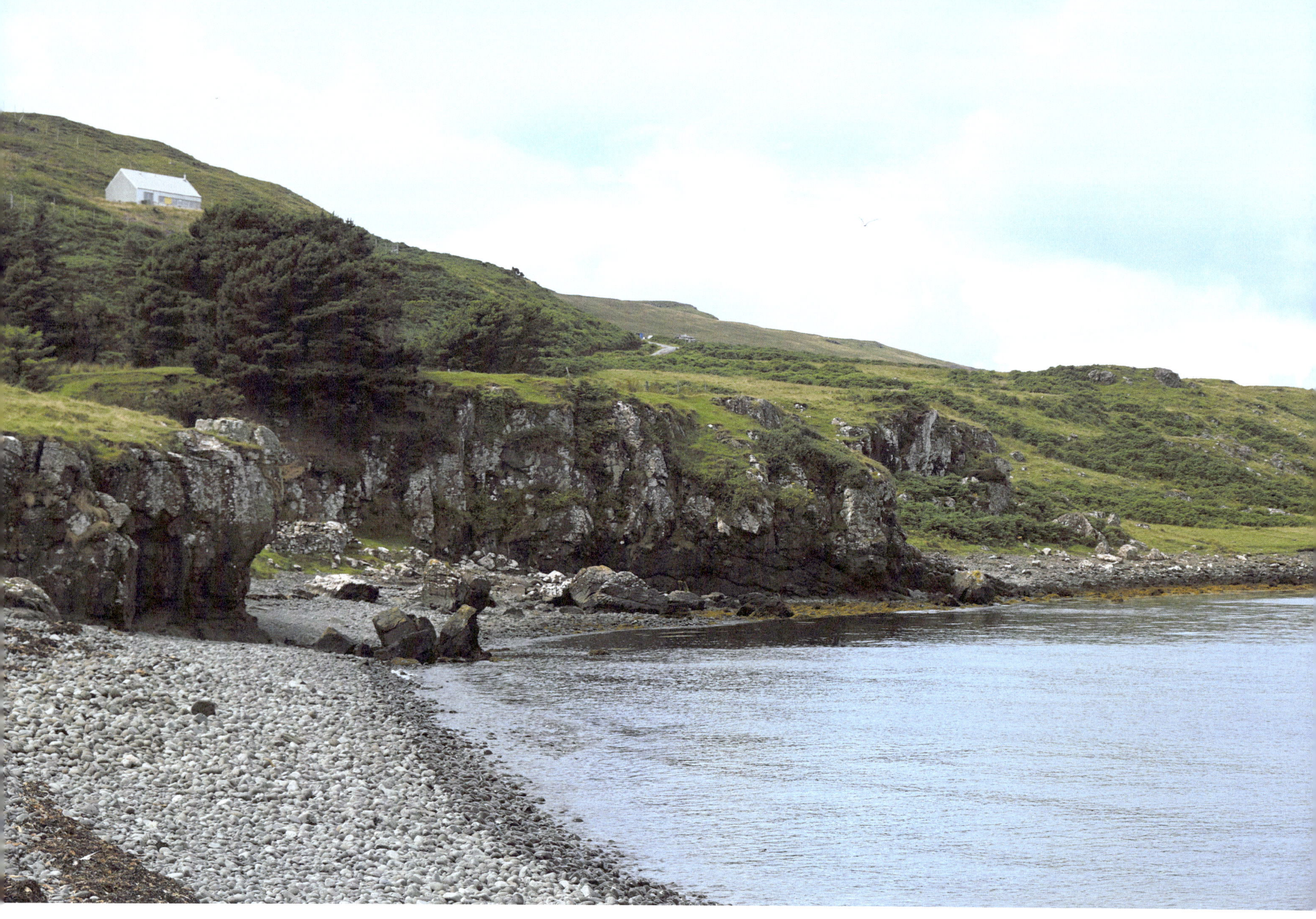

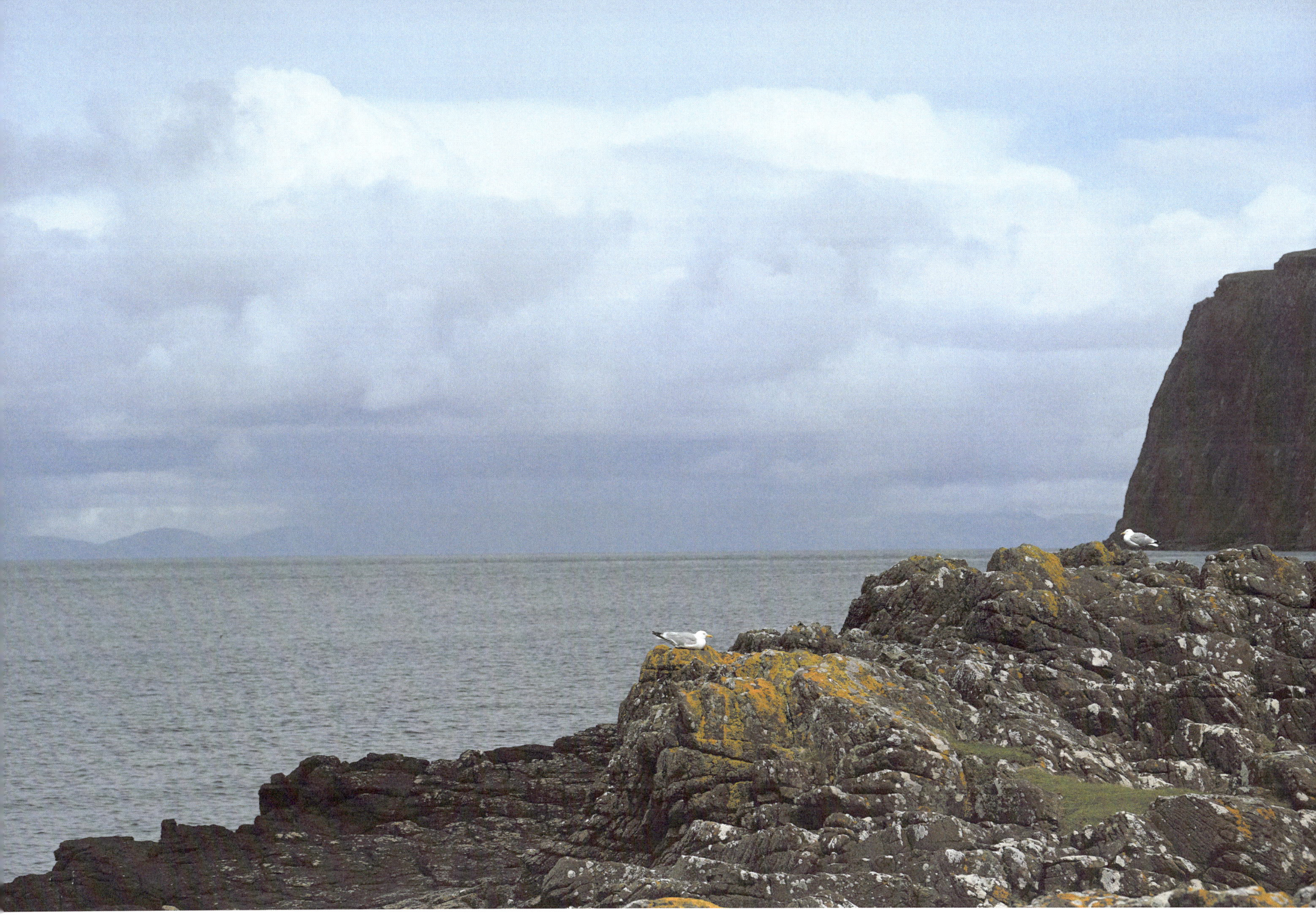

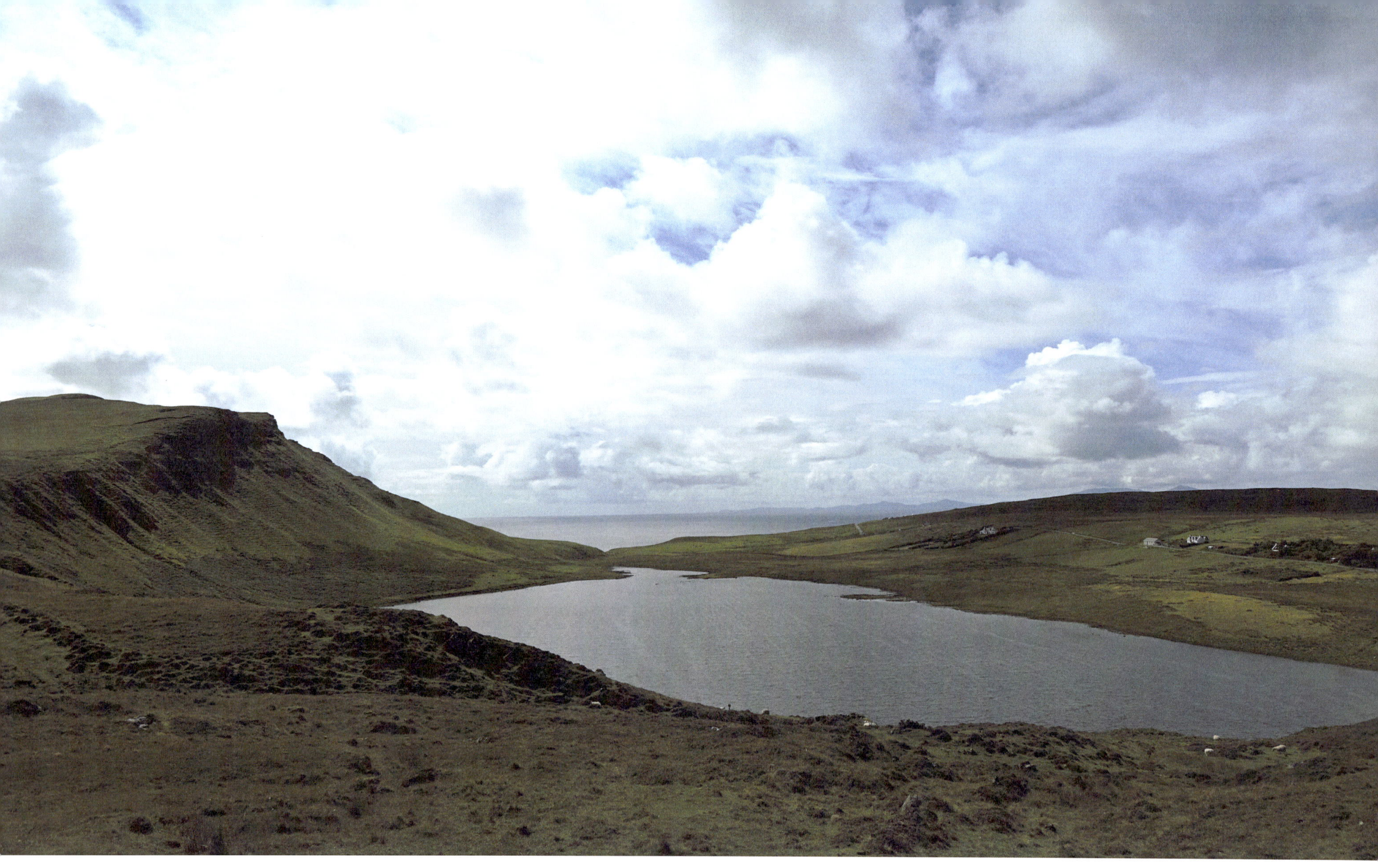

Our host directed us to the breathtaking views of Neist Point. We weren't disappointed, but, as it was summer, American, Australian and European tourists arrived in their droves to admire the view and in search of whales.

No wonder the island is so popular. Skye is a place of strange and rugged rock formations and waterfalls, of castles and fishing villages. It has a rich history of clan battles, of the Jacobite Rising and Highland Clearances. I know we will return.

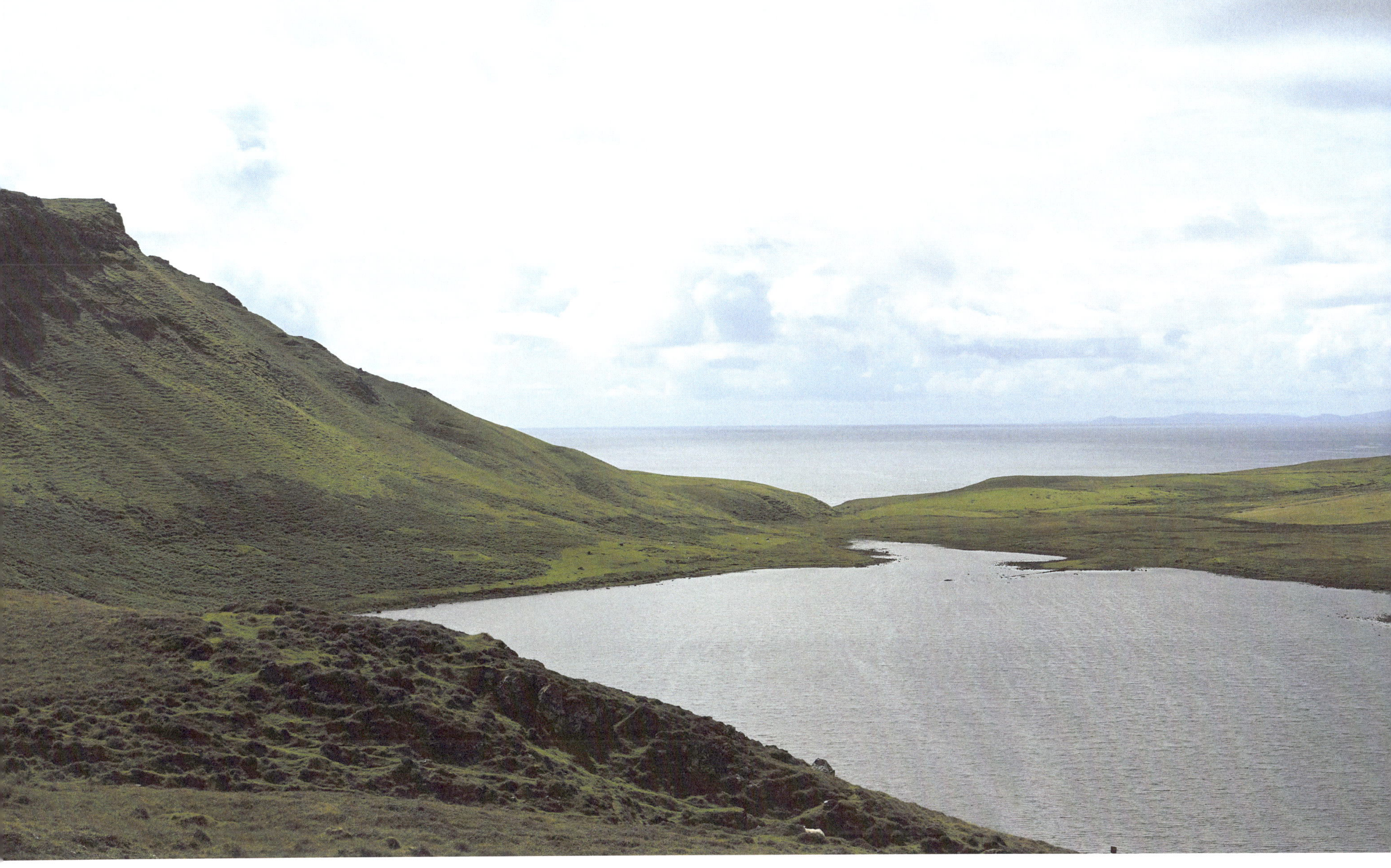

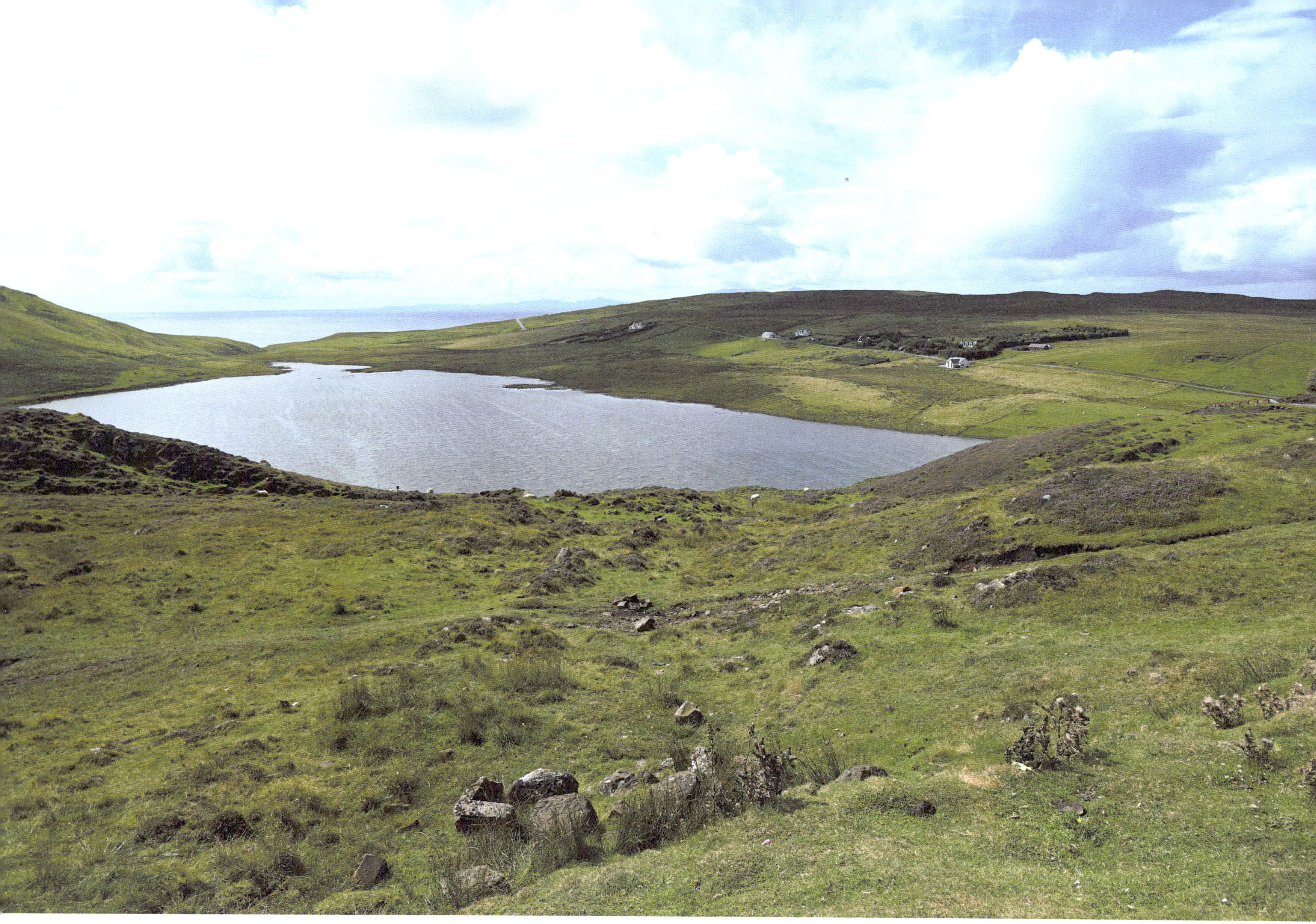

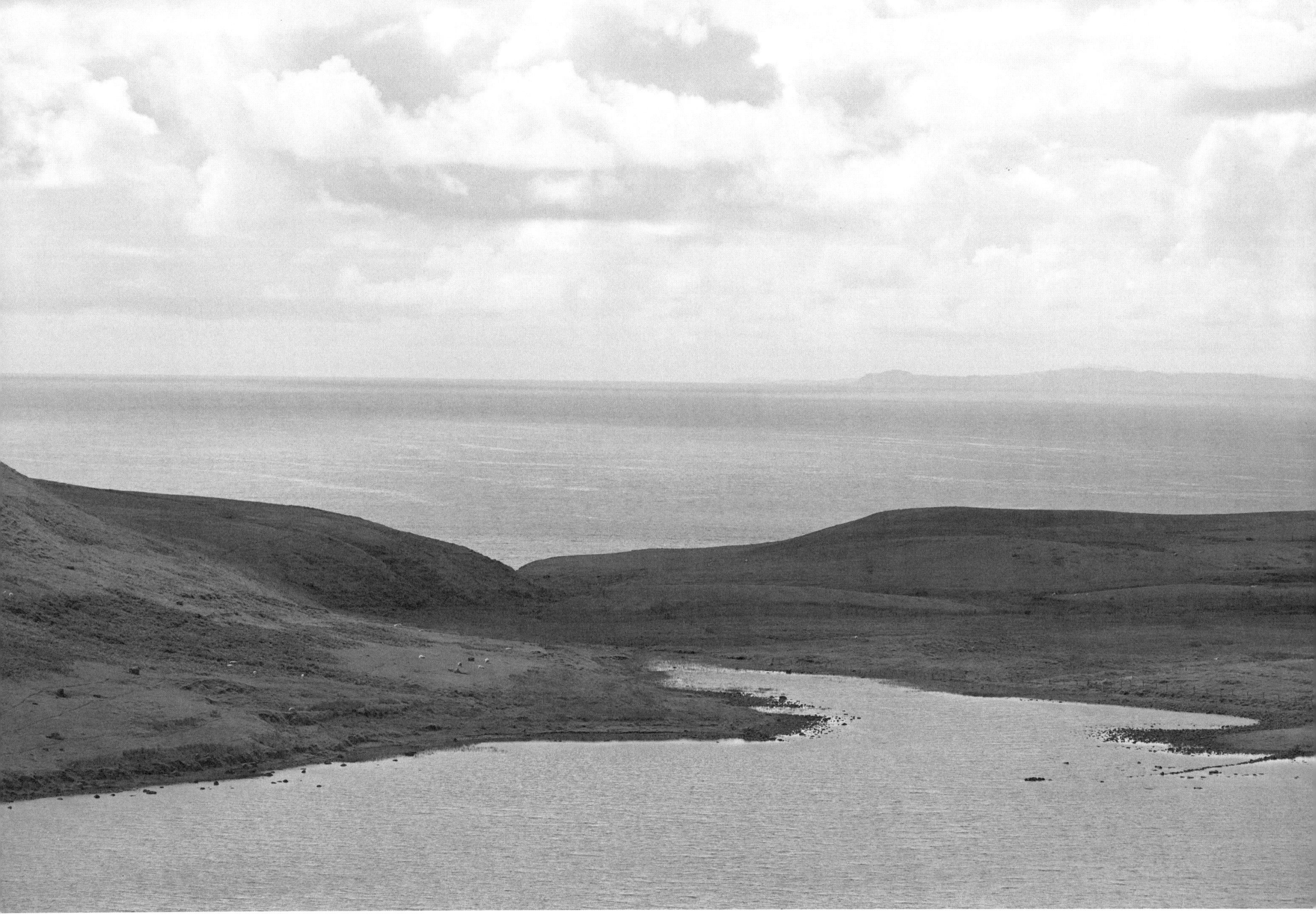

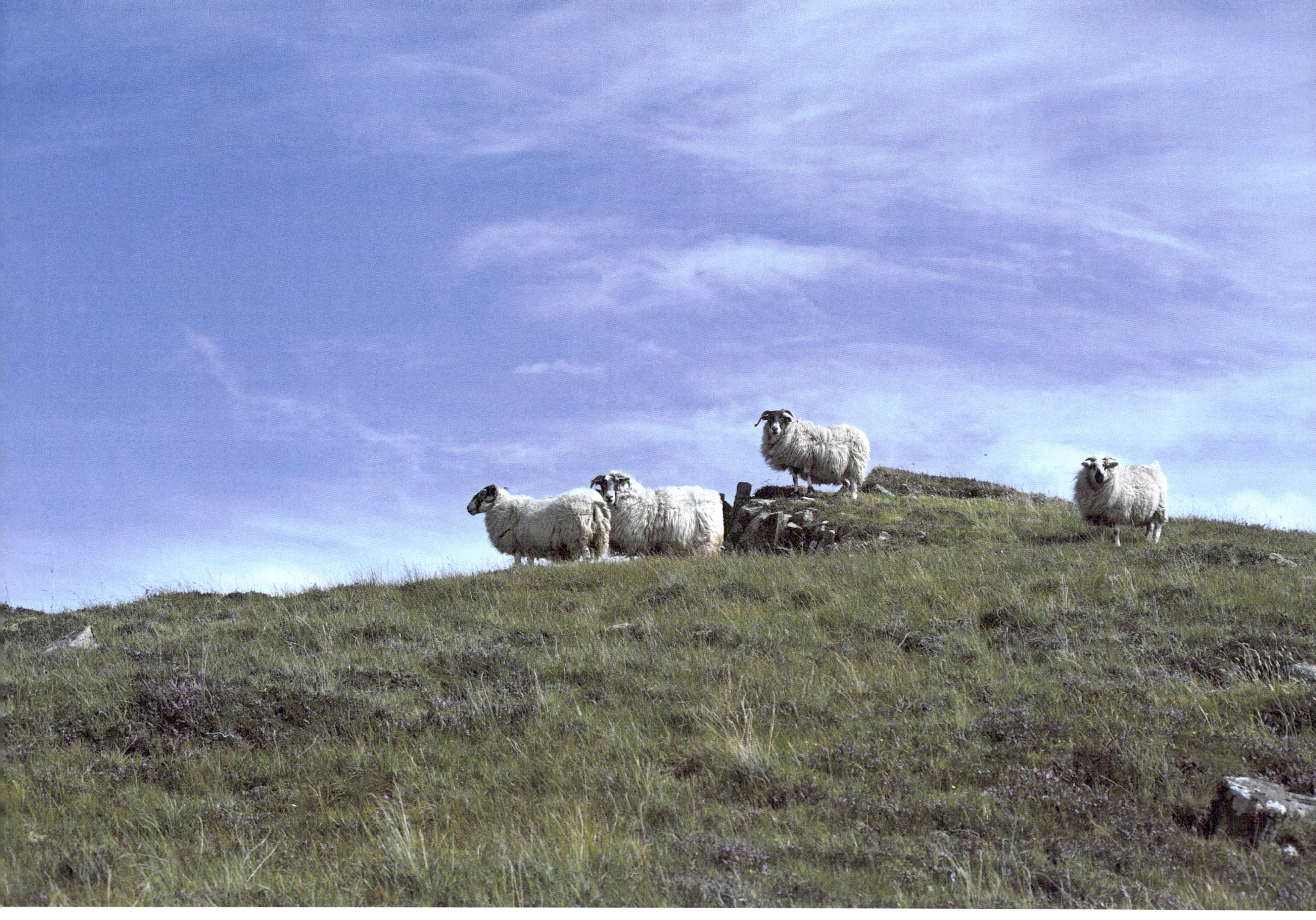

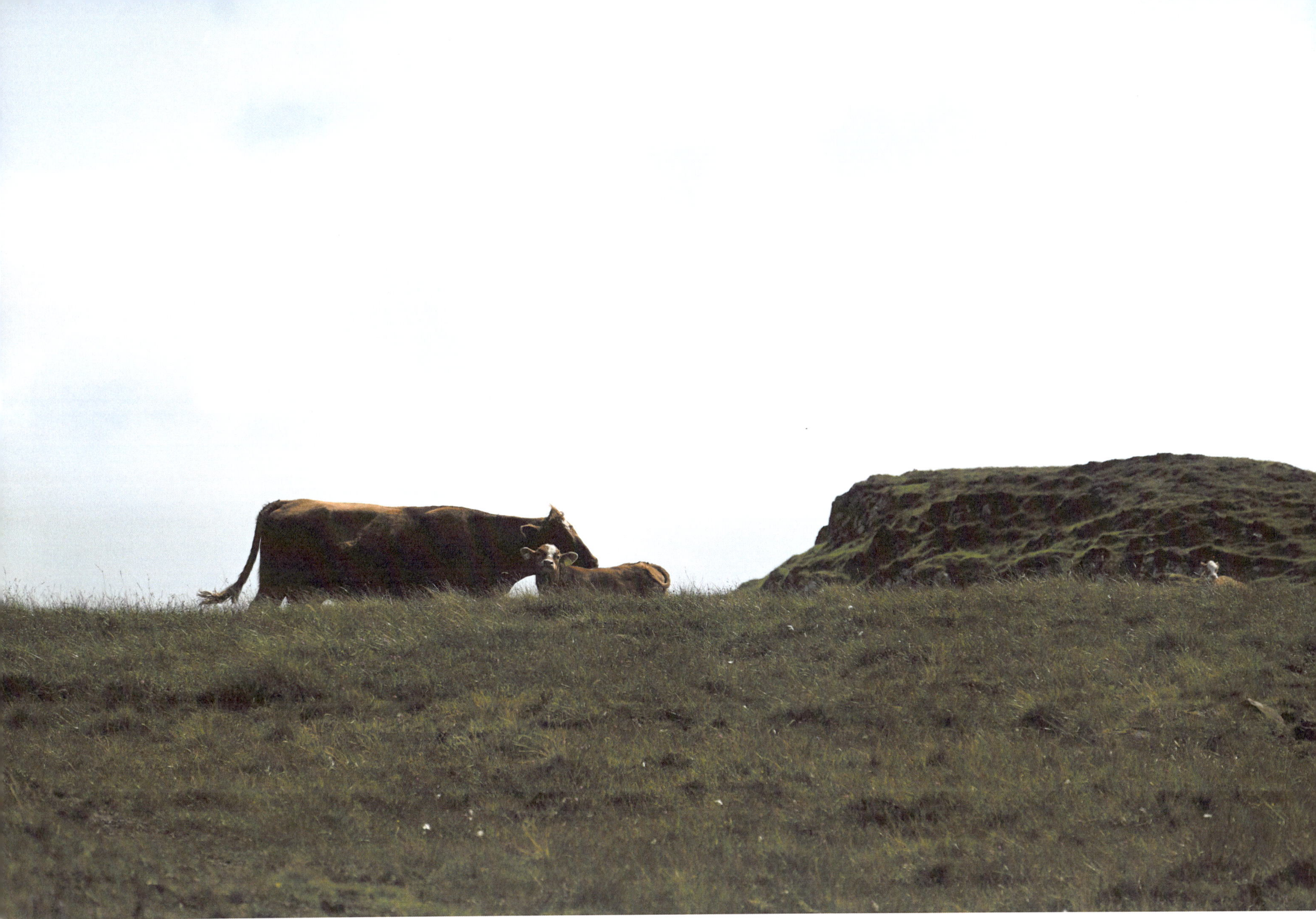

Milton Keynes UK
Ingram Content Group UK Ltd.
UKRC042110260124
436760UK00002B/6

* 9 7 8 1 8 0 3 8 1 7 6 5 1 *